James Barnes

**Naval Actions of the War of 1812**

James Barnes

**Naval Actions of the War of 1812**

ISBN/EAN: 9783744653190

Printed in Europe, USA, Canada, Australia, Japan

Cover: Foto ©ninafisch / pixelio.de

More available books at **www.hansebooks.com**

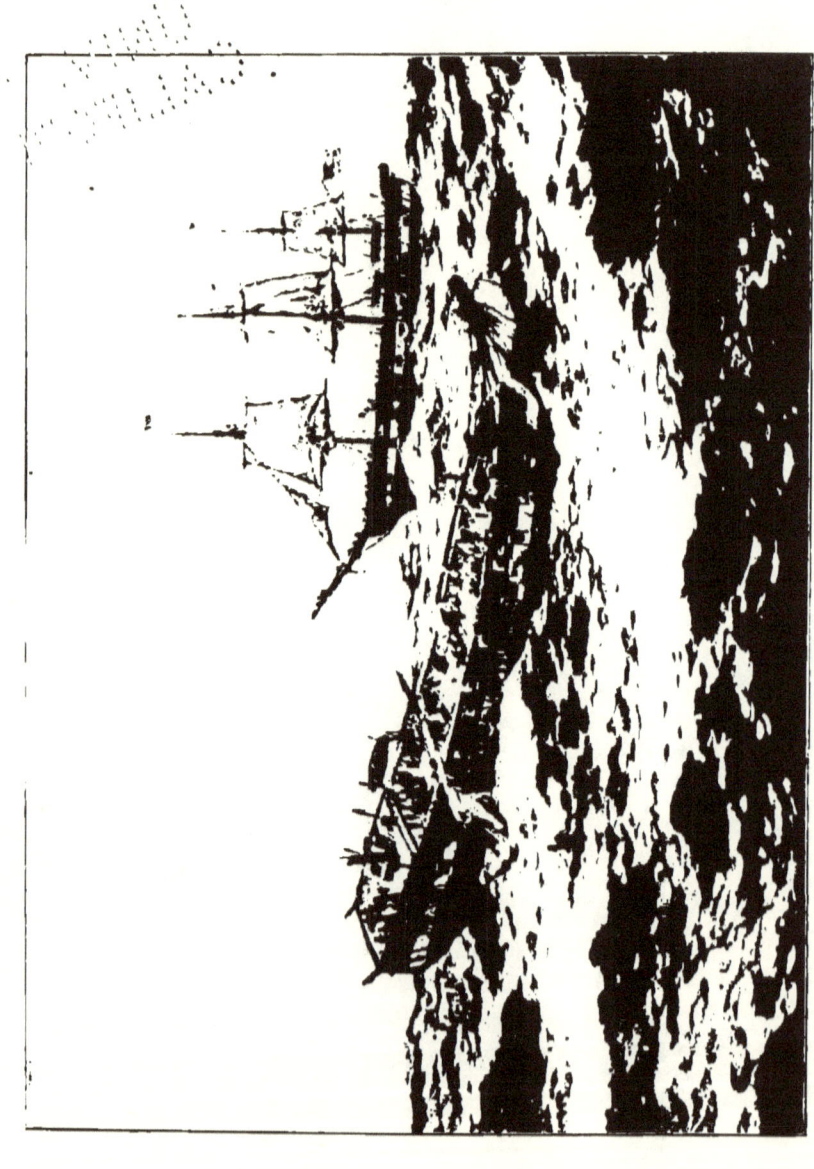

# NAVAL ACTIONS

OF

# THE WAR OF 1812

BY
JAMES BARNES
AUTHOR OF
"FOR KING OR COUNTRY"

WITH ILLUSTRATIONS BY
CARLTON T. CHAPMAN

NEW YORK
HARPER & BROTHERS PUBLISHERS

## BY THE SAME AUTHOR.

**FOR KING OR COUNTRY.** A Story of the American Revolution. Illustrated. Post 8vo, Cloth, $1 50.

A story that will be eagerly welcomed by boys of all ages. . . . It is doubtful whether the reader will be content to lay the story aside until he has finished it. It is a good book for an idle day in the country, and we cordially recommend it both to boys on a holiday and to boys that stay at home.—*Saturday Evening Gazette*, Boston.

A spirited story of the days that tried men's souls, full of incident and movement that keep up the reader's interest to the turning of the last page. It is full of dramatic situations and graphic descriptions which irresistibly lead the reader on, regretful at the close that there is not still more of it.—*Christian Work*, N. Y.

A fascinating study. It is replete with those Homeric touches which delight the heart of the healthy boy. . . . It would be difficult to find a more fascinating book for the young.—*Philadelphia Bulletin.*

A capital story for boys, both young and old; full of adventure and movement, thoroughly patriotic in tone, throwing luminous sidelights upon the main events of the Revolution.—*Brooklyn Standard-Union.*

PUBLISHED BY HARPER & BROTHERS, NEW YORK.

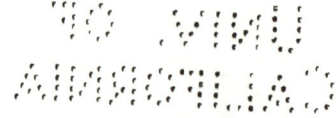

Copyright, 1896, by HARPER & BROTHERS.

TO
## MY FATHER
WHOSE ENCOURAGEMENT AND ASSISTANCE ARE HEREBY
ACKNOWLEDGED WITH AFFECTIONATE GRATITUDE
I HAVE THE HONOR TO DEDICATE
**THIS BOOK**

# PREFACE

THE country that has no national heroes whose deeds should be found emblazoned on her annals, that can boast no men whose lives and conduct can be held up as examples of what loyalty, valor, and courage should be, that country has no patriotism, no heart, no soul.

If it be wrong to tell of a glorious past, for fear of keeping alive an animosity that should have perished with time, there have been many offenders; and the author of the following pages thus writes himself down as one of them. Truly, if pride in the past be a safeguard for the future in forming a national spirit, America should rejoice.

There exists no Englishman to-day whose heart is not moved at the word "Trafalgar," or whose feelings are not stirred by the sentence "England expects every man to do his duty." The slight, one-armed figure of Admiral Nelson has been before the Briton's eyes as boy and man, surrounded always with the glamour that will never cease to enshroud a nation's hero. Has it kept alive a feeling of animosity against France to dwell on such a man as this, and to keep his deeds alive? So it may be. But no Englishman would hide the cause in order to lose the supposed effect of it.

In searching the history of our own country, when it stood together as a united nation, waging just war, we find England, our mother country, whose language we speak, arrayed against us. But, on account of this bond of birth and language, should we cease to tell about the deeds of those men who freed us from her grasp and oppressions, and made us what we are? I trust not. May our navy glory in its record, no matter the consequences! May our youth grow up with the lives of these men—our Yankee commanders—before them, and may they profit by their examples!

This should not inculcate a hatred for a former foe. It should only serve to build up that national *esprit de corps* without which no country ever stood up for its rights and willed to fight for them. May the sons of our new citizens, whose fathers have served kings, perhaps, and come from other countries, grow up with a pride in America's own national history! How can this be given them unless they read of it in books or gain it from teaching?

But it is not the intention to instruct that has caused the author to compile and collate the material used in the following pages. He has been influenced by his own feelings, that are shared by the many thousands of the descendants of " the men who fought." It has been his pleasure, and this alone is his excuse.

Mr. Carlton T. Chapman, whose spirited paintings are reproduced to illustrate this volume, has caught the atmosphere of action, and has given us back the old days in a way that makes us feel them.

# CONTENTS

                                                        PAGE

INTRODUCTION . . . . . . . . . . . . . . . . . 1

## I

The United States frigate *Constitution*, on July 17th, 1812, falls in with a British squadron, but escapes, owing to the masterly seamanship of Captain Isaac Hull . . . . . 23

## II

The *Constitution*, under command of Captain Hull, captures the British frigate *Guerrière*, under command of Captain Richard Dacres, August 19th, 1812 . . . . . . . . . 35

## III

The United States sloop of war *Wasp*, Captain Jacob Jones, captures the English sloop of war *Frolic*, October 18th, 1812; both vessels taken on the same day by the English seventy-four *Poictiers* . . . . . . . . . . . . . . 47

## IV

October 25th, 1812, the British frigate *Macedonian*, commanded by John S. Carden, is captured by the *United States* frigate, under command of Stephen Decatur; the prize is brought to port . . . . . . . . . . . . . . 59

## V

Captain Wm. Bainbridge, in the *Constitution*, captures the British frigate *Java* off the coast of Brazil, December 29th, 1812; the *Java* is set fire to and blows up. . . . 73

## VI

Gallant action of the privateer schooner *Comet*, of 14 guns, against three English vessels and one Portuguese, January 14th, 1813 . . . . . . . . . . . . . . . . . 91

## VII

The United States sloop of war *Hornet*, Captain James Lawrence, takes the British brig *Peacock;* the latter sinks after the action, February 24th, 1813 . . . . . . . . . 103

## VIII

The United States frigate *Chesapeake* is captured by the English frigate *Shannon* after a gallant defence, June 1st, 1813 . . . . . . . . . . . . . . . . . . . . . . 113

## IX

The United States brig *Enterprise*, commanded by William Burrows, captures H. B. M. sloop of war *Boxer*, September 5th, 1813; Burrows killed during the action . . . 129

## X

On September 10th, 1813, the American fleet on Lake Erie, under the command of Oliver Hazard Perry, captures the entire English naval force under Commodore Barclay. . . . . . . . . . . . . . . . . . . . . . . . 139

## XI

The American privateer brig *General Armstrong*, of 9 guns and 90 men, repulses a boat attack in the harbor of Fayal, the British suffering a terrific loss, September 27th, 1813 . . . . . . . . . . . . . . . . . . 159

## XII

March 28th, 1814, the United States frigate *Essex*, under Captain David Porter, is captured by two English vessels, the *Phœbe* and the *Cherub*, in the harbor of Valparaiso . 171

## XIII

The United States sloop of war *Peacock*, commanded by Captain Warrington, takes the British sloop of war *L'Epervier* on April 29th, 1814 . . . . . . . . . . . . . 191

## XIV

The United States sloop of war *Wasp*, under command of Captain Blakeley, captures the British sloop of war *Reindeer*, June 28th, 1814. The *Wasp* engages the British sloop of war *Avon* on the 1st of September; the English vessel sinks after the *Wasp* is driven off by a superior force . 199

## XV

September 11th, the American forces on Lake Champlain, under Captain Macdonough, capture the English squadron, under Captain Downey, causing the evacuation of New York State by the British. . . . . . . . . . . . . 209

## XVI

The United States frigate *President*, under command of Captain Decatur, is taken by a British squadron after a long chase, during which the *President* completely disabled one of her antagonists, January 15th, 1815. . . . . . 219

## XVII

February 20th, 1815, the *Constitution*, under Captain Stewart, engages and captures two English vessels that prove to be the *Cyane* and the *Levant;* one of her prizes is retaken, and the *Constitution* again has a narrow escape . . . . 231

## XVIII

The British brig of war *Penguin* surrenders to the United States brig *Hornet*, commanded by Captain James Biddle; the *Penguin* sinks immediately after the accident, March 23d, 1815 . . . . . . . . . . . . . . . 245

## XIX

The chase of the *Hornet*, sloop of war, by the *Cornwallis*, a British line-of-battle ship. . . . . . . . . . . . 255

# ILLUSTRATIONS

| | |
|---|---|
| THE SURRENDER OF THE "GUERRIÈRE" . . . . . | *Frontispiece* |
| MEDAL PRESENTED BY CONGRESS TO CAPTAIN ISAAC HULL | *Facing p.* 22 |
| THE "CONSTITUTION" TOWING AND KEDGING . . . . | " 26 |
| THE "WASP" RAKING THE "FROLIC" . . . . . . | " 50 |
| MEDAL PRESENTED BY CONGRESS TO CAPTAIN STEPHEN DECATUR . . . . . . . . . . . . . | " 58 |
| MEDAL PRESENTED BY CONGRESS TO CAPTAIN WILLIAM BAINBRIDGE . . . . . . . . . . . . | " 72 |
| MEDAL PRESENTED BY CONGRESS TO CAPTAIN JAMES LAWRENCE . . . . . . . . . . . . . | " 102 |
| THE "PEACOCK" AND "HORNET" AT CLOSE QUARTERS | " 106 |
| THE "CHESAPEAKE" LEAVING THE HARBOR . . . . | " 116 |
| MEMORIAL MEDAL IN HONOR OF CAPTAIN WILLIAM BURROWS . . . . . . . . . . . . . . | " 128 |
| MEDAL PRESENTED BY CONGRESS TO LIEUTENANT EDWARD R. McCALL . . . . . . . . . . . | " 128 |
| THE "ENTERPRISE" HULLING THE "BOXER" . . . . | " 132 |
| MEDAL PRESENTED BY CONGRESS TO CAPTAIN OLIVER HAZARD PERRY . . . . . . . . . . . | " 138 |
| THE "NIAGARA" BREAKS THE ENGLISH LINE . . . . | " 148 |
| THE "ESSEX" BEING CUT TO PIECES . . . . . . | " 184 |
| MEDAL PRESENTED BY CONGRESS TO CAPTAIN LEWIS WARRINGTON . . . . . . . . . . . . | " 190 |

| | |
|---|---|
| THE "PEACOCK" CAPTURES THE "EPERVIER" | Facing p. 192 |
| MEDAL PRESENTED BY CONGRESS TO CAPTAIN JOHNSTON BLAKELEY | " 198 |
| THE "WASP'S" FIGHT WITH THE "AVON" | " 204 |
| MEDAL PRESENTED BY CONGRESS TO CAPTAIN THOMAS MACDONOUGH | " 208 |
| THE "PRESIDENT" ENDEAVORING TO ESCAPE | " 222 |
| MEDAL PRESENTED BY CONGRESS TO CAPTAIN CHARLES STEWART | " 230 |
| THE "CONSTITUTION" TAKING THE "CYANE" | " 236 |
| MEDAL PRESENTED BY CONGRESS TO CAPTAIN JAMES BIDDLE | " 244 |
| THE "PENGUIN" STRIKES TO THE "HORNET" | " 252 |

# INTRODUCTION

To study the condition of affairs that led up to the declaration of the second war against Great Britain we have but to turn to the sea. Although England, it must be confessed, had plenty of fighting on her hands and troubles enough at home, she had not forgotten the chagrin and disappointments caused by the loss of the American colonies through a mistaken enforcement of high-handedness. And it was this same tendency that brought to her vaunted and successful navy as great an overthrow as their arms had received on land some thirty-seven years previously.

The impressment of American seamen into the English service had been continued despite remonstrances from our government, until the hatred for the sight of the cross of St. George that stirred the hearts of Yankee sailormen had passed all bounds. America under these conditions developed a type of patriot seafarer, and this fact may account for his manners under fire and his courage in all circumstances.

The United States was an outboard country, so

to speak. We had no great interstate traffic, no huge, developed West to draw upon, to exchange and barter with. Our people thronged the sea-coast, and vessels made of American pine and live-oak were manned by *American men.* They had sought their calling by choice, and not by compulsion. They had not been driven from crowded cities because they could not live there. They had not been taken from peaceful homes and wives and children by press-gangs, as was the English custom, to slave on board the great vessels that Great Britain kept afloat by such means, and such alone. But of his own free-will the Yankee sailor sought the sea, and of his own free-will he served his country. It would be useless to deny that the greater liberty, the higher pay, the large chance for reward, tempted many foreigners and many ex-servants of the king to cast their lot with us. But when we think that there were kept unwillingly on English vessels of war almost as many American seamen as were giving voluntary service to their country in our little navy, we can see on which side the great proportion lies.

It is easy to see that the American mind was a pent furnace. It only needed a few more evidences of England's injustice and contempt to make the press and public speech roar with hatred and cry out for revenge. So when in June, 1812, war was declared against Great Britain, it was hailed with approbation and delight. But shots had been exchanged before this, and there were men who knew the value of seamanship, recognized the fact that every shot must tell, that every man must be ready, and that to the navy the country looked; for the idea of a great invasion by England was scouted. It was a war for the rights of sailors, the freedom of the high-seas, and the grand and never thread-worn principles of liberty.

So wide-spread had been the patriotism of our citizens during the revolutionary war that our only frigates, except those made up of aged merchant-vessels, had been built by private subscription; but now the government was awake, alert, and able.

To take just a glance at the condition of affairs that led up to this is of great interest.

So far back as the year 1798 the impositions of Great Britain upon our merchantmen are on record, and on November 16th of that year they culminated in a deliberate outrage and insult to our flag.

The U. S. ship of war *Baltimore*, of 20 guns, was overhauled by a British squadron, and five American seamen were impressed from the crew. At this time we were engaged in the quasi-war with France, during which the *Constellation*, under Captain Truxton, captured the French frigate *L'Insurgent*, of 54 guns. On February 1st, 1800, a year after the first action, the same vessel, under the same commander, captured *La Vengeance*, of 54 guns. On October 12th of the same year the U. S. frigate *Boston* captured the French corvette *Le Berceau*. Minor actions between the French privateers and our merchantmen occurred constantly. We lost but one of our national vessels, however—the schooner *Retaliation*, captured by two French frigates.

England was protecting the Barbary pirates in the Mediterranean at this time, in order to keep out competitive commerce — a fine bit of business! Europe and America bought immunity.

On June 10th, 1801, war was declared, however, by the Bashaw of Tripoli against the United States, because we failed to accede to his demands for larger tribute, and a brief summary of the conduct of this war will show plainly that here our officers had chances to distinguish themselves, and the American seamen won distinction in foreign waters.

Captain Bainbridge, in command of the frigate *Philadelphia*, late in August, 1803, captured off the Cape de Gatt a Moorish cruiser, and retook her prize, an American brig. About two months later the *Philadelphia*, in chase of one of the corsairs, ran on a reef of rocks under the guns of a battery, and after four hours' action Bainbridge was compelled to strike his flag to the Tripolitans. For months, now, it was the single aim of the American squadron under Preble to destroy the *Philadelphia*, in order to prevent her being used against the United States, and on February 15th, 1804, this was successfully accomplished by Lieutenant Stephen Decatur and seventy volunteers, who entered the harbor on the ketch *Intrepid*, set fire to the *Philadelphia*, and escaped.

All through August Preble's squadron hovered about the harbor of Tripoli, and bombarded the town on four separate occasions. On June 3d, 1805, he arranged a peace with the Tripolitans, and two days later Bainbridge and the American prisoners were liberated. But the bashaw could not control the piratical cruisers who made his harbor a rendezvous, and in September hostilities were again commenced, during which occurred the sad accident, the premature blowing up of the fire ship *Intrepid*, by which the navy lost Captain Richard Somers, one of its bravest officers, two lieutenants, and ten seamen.

But to return to the relations existing between America and England. A crisis was fast approaching. Off the shore of Maryland on June 22d, 1807, the crowning outrage attending England's self-assumed "right of search" took place, when the British sloop of war *Leopard*, 50 guns, fired upon the *Chesapeake*, 36 guns, which vessel, under command of Captain Barron, had just shipped a green crew, and could return, owing to her unprepared condition, but one shot to the Englishman's broadside. Barron hauled down his flag, and had to allow himself to be searched by the orders of Captain Humphries, commander of the *Leopard*, and four American-born seamen were taken out of his crew and sent on board the Englishman. It was claimed by Captain Humphries that three of these men were deserters from the British frigate *Melampus*. Although the *Chesapeake* had hauled down her flag and surrendered, the *Leopard* paid no attention to this, and sailed away, leaving Barron with three men killed and eighteen wounded, and his ship badly damaged in hull, spars, and rigging. Barron was censured by a court of inquiry and suspended from his command. Looking at this sentence dispassionately, it was most unjust.

But the indignation that was felt throughout the country over this affair wrought the temper of the people to a fever-heat. Congress passed resolutions, and the President of the United States issued a proclamation, forbidding all British armed vessels from entering the ports of the United States, and prohibiting all inhabitants of the United States from furnishing them with supplies of any description.

Great Britain's disavowal of the act of Admiral Berkeley (under whose command Captain Humphries had acted) was lukewarm, and the Admiral's trial was something of a farce, and gave little satisfaction to America.

Napoleon at about this time had begun his senseless closing of French ports to American vessels, and once more the French cruisers apparently considered all Yankee craft their proper prey. They would interrupt and take from them stores, water, or whatever they considered necessary, without remuneration or apology. As the English were taking our seamen and showing absolute contempt for our flag wherever found, the condition of our merchant marine was most precarious. No vessel felt secure upon the high seas, and yet the English merchant ships continued to ply their trade with us.

On May 1st, 1810, all French and English vessels of any description were prohibited from entering the ports of the United States. On June 24th of this year the British sloop of war *Moselle* fired at the U. S. brig *Vixen*, off the Bahamas, but fortunately did no damage. Another blow to American commerce just at this period was the closing of the ports of Prussia to American products and ships. But an event which took place on May 16th, 1811, had an unexpected termination that turned all eyes to England. The British frigate *Guerrière* was one of a fleet of English vessels hanging about our coasts, and cruising mainly along the New Jersey and Long Island shores. Commodore Rodgers was proceeding from Annapolis to New York in the *President*, 44 guns, when the news was brought to him by a coasting vessel that a young man, a native of New Jersey, had been taken from an American brig in the vicinity of Sandy Hook, and had been carried off by a frigate supposed to be the *Guerrière*. On the 16th, about noon, Rodgers discovered a sail standing towards him. She was made out to be a man-of-war, and concluding that she was the *Guerrière*, the commodore resolved to speak to her, and, to quote from a contemporary, " he hoped he might prevail upon her commander to release the impressed young man" (what arguments he intended to use are not stated). But no sooner had the stranger perceived the *President*, whose colors were flying, than she wore and stood to the southward. Rodgers took after her, and by evening was close enough to make out that she was beyond all doubt an English ship. But owing to the dusk and thick weather it was impossible to count her broadside, or to make out distinctly what was the character of the flag that at this late hour she had hoisted at her peak. So he determined to lay his vessel alongside of her within speaking distance, and find out something definite. The strange sail apparently wished to avoid this if possible, and tacked and manœuvred incessantly in efforts to escape. At twenty minutes past eight the *President*, being a little forward of the weather beam of the chase, and within a hundred yards of her, Rodgers called through his trumpet with the usual hail, "What ship is that?" No answer was given, but the question was repeated from the other vessel in turn. Rodgers did not answer, and hailed again. To his intense surprise a shot was fired into the *President*, and this was the only response. A great deal of controversy resulted from the subsequent happenings. The English deny having fired the first gun, and assert that Rodgers was the offender, as a gun was discharged (without orders) from the American vessel almost at the same moment. Now a brisk action commenced with broadsides and musketry. But the commodore, noticing that he was having to deal with a very inferior force, ceased firing, after about ten minutes of exchanging shots. He was premature in this, however, as the other vessel immediately renewed her fire, and the foremast of the *President* was badly injured by two thirty-two-pound shot. By this time the wind had blown up fresh, and there was a heavy sea; but notwithstanding this fact and the growing darkness, a well-directed broadside from the *President* silenced the other's fire completely. Rodgers approached again, and to his hail this time there was given some reply. Owing to his being to windward, he did not catch the words, although he understood from them that his antagonist was a British ship. All night long Rodgers lay hove to under the lee of the stranger, displaying lights, and ready at any moment to respond to any call for assistance, as it had been perceived that the smaller vessel was badly crippled.

At daylight the *President* bore down to within speaking distance and an easy sail, and Rodgers sent out his first cutter, under command of Lieutenant Creighton, to learn the name of the ship and her commander, and with instructions to ascertain what damage she had received, and to "regret the necessity which had led to such an unhappy result." Lieutenant Creighton returned with the information that the British captain declined accepting any assistance, and that the vessel was His Britannic Majesty's sloop of war *Little Belt*, 18 guns. She had nine men killed and twenty-two wounded. No one was killed on board the *President*, and only a cabin-boy had been wounded in the arm by a splinter.

The account given to his government by Captain Bingham, of the *Little Belt*, gives the lie direct to the sworn statement of the affair, confirmed by all the officers and crew of the *President*, an account, by-the-way, that after a long and minute investigation was sustained by the American courts. It was now past doubting that open war would shortly follow between this country and England. Preparations immediately began in every large city to outfit privateers, and the navy-yards rang with hammers, and the recruiting officers were besieged by hordes of sailormen anxious to serve a gun and seek revenge.

Owing to circumstances, the year of 1812, that gave the name to the war of the next three years, found the country in a peculiar condition. Under the "gunboat system" of Mr. Jefferson, who believed in harbor protection, and trusted to escape war, an act had been passed in 1805 which almost threatened annihilation of a practical navy. The construction of twenty-five gunboats authorized by this bill had been followed, from time to time, by the building of more of them under the mistaken idea that this policy was a national safeguard. They would have been of great use as a branch of coast fortification at that time, it may be true, but they were absolutely of no account in the prosecution of a war at sea. Up to the year 1811 in the neighborhood of two hundred of these miserable vessels had been constructed, and they lay about the harbors in various conditions of uselessness.

From an official statement it appears that there were but three first-class frigates in our navy, and that but five vessels of any description were in condition to go to sea. They were the *President*, 44 guns; the *United States*, 44 guns; the *Constitution*, 44 guns; the *Essex*, 32 guns; and the *Congress*, 36 guns. All of our sea-going craft taken together were but ten in number, and seven of these were of the second class and of inferior armament. There was not a single ship that did not need extensive repairs, and two of the smaller frigates, the *New York* and the *Boston*, were condemned upon examination. The navy was in a deplorable state, and no money forthcoming.

But the session of Congress known as the "war session" altered this state of affairs, and in the act of March 13th, 1812, we find the repudiation of the gunboat policy, and the ridiculous error advanced, to our shame be it said, by some members of Congress, that "in creating a navy we are only building ships for Great Britain," was cast aside. Not only did the act provide for putting the frigates into commission and preparing them for actual service, but two hundred thousand dollars per annum was appropriated for three years for ship timber. The gunboats were laid up "for the good of the public service," and disappeared. Up to this period all the acts of Congress in favor of the navy had been but to make hasty preparations of a few vessels of war to meet the pressure of some emergency, but no permanent footing had been established. The conduct and the result of the war with Tripoli had not been such as to make the American navy popular, despite the individual brave deeds that had taken place and the respect for the flag that had been enforced abroad. But the formation of a "naval committee" was a step in the right direction. There was a crisis to be met, the country was awake to the necessity, and the feelings of patriotism had aroused the authorities to a pitch of action. Many men, the ablest in the country, were forced into public life from their retirement, and a combination was presented in the House of Representatives and in the Senate that promised well for the conduct of affairs. The Republican party saw that there was no more sense in the system of restriction, and that the only way to redress the wrongs of our sailors was by war.

Langdon Cheves was appointed chairman of this Committee of Naval Affairs of the Twelfth Congress, and took hold of the work assigned to him with energy and judgment. There was some slight opposition given by people who doubted our power and resources to wage war successfully against Great Britain, but this opposition was overwhelmed completely at the outset. The report of the naval committee shows that the naval establishments of other countries had been carefully looked into, and experienced and intelligent officers had been called upon for assistance; that the needs and resources of the country had been accurately determined, and the result was that the committee expressed the opinion "*that it was the true policy of the United States to build up a navy establishment as the cheapest, the safest, and the best protection to their seacoast and to their commerce, and that such an establishment was inseparably connected with the future prosperity, safety, and glory of the country.*"

The bill which was introduced and drafted by the committee recommended that the force to be created should consist of frigates and sloops of war to be built at once, and that those already in commission be overhauled and refitted. To quote from the first bill for the increase of the navy, communicated to the House of Representatives September 17th, 1811 (which antedated the final act of March 13th, 1812), Mr. Cheves says for the committee: "We beg leave to recommend that all the vessels of war of the United States not now in service, which are worthy of repair, be immediately repaired, fitted out, and put into actual service; that ten additional frigates, averaging 38 guns, be built; that a competent sum of money be appropriated for the purchase of a stock of timber, and that a dock for repairing the vessels of war of the United States be established in some central and convenient place." There was no dock in the country at this date, and vessels had to be "hove down" to repair their hulls—an expensive and lengthy process.

A large number of experiments had also been made during this year in reference to the practical use of the torpedo. They were conducted in the city and harbor of New York, under the supervision of Oliver Walcott, John Kent, Cadwallader B. Colden, John Garnet, and Jonathan Williams. Suggestions were also made for the defence of vessels threatened by torpedo attack in much the same method that is employed to this date—by nets and booms. Mr. Colden says in a letter addressed to Paul Hamilton, Secretary of the Navy, in reference to the experiments with Mr. Fulton's torpedoes, "I cannot but think that if the dread of torpedoes were to produce no other effect than to induce every hostile vessel of war which enters our ports to protect herself in a way in which the *Argus* (the vessel experimented with) was protected, torpedoes will be no inconsiderable auxiliaries in the defence of our harbors." Strange to say, a boom torpedo rigged to the end of a boom attached to the prow of a cutter propelled by oars was tried, and is to this day adopted in our service, in connection with fast steam-launches. All this tends to show the advancing interest in naval warfare. Paul Hamilton suggested, in a letter dated December 3d, 1811, that "a naval force of twelve sails of the line (74's) and twenty well-constructed frigates, including those already in commission, would be ample to protect the coasting trade"; but there was no provision in the bill as finally accepted, and no authority given for the construction of any line of battle ships, although Mr. Cheves referred in his speech to the letter from Secretary Hamilton. Plans were also made this year to form a naval hospital, a much-needed institution.

When war was declared by Congress against Great Britain, on June 18th, 1812, and proclaimed by the President of the United States the following day, the number of vessels, exclusive of those projected and building, was as follows:

### FRIGATES

| | Rated | Mounting | Commanders |
|---|---|---|---|
| *Constitution* . . . . | 44 | 56 | Capt. Hull |
| *United States* . . . | 44 | 56 | Capt. Decatur |
| *President* . . . . . | 44 | 56 | Com. Rodgers |
| *Chesapeake* . . . . | 36 | 44 | Capt. Evans |
| *New York* . . . . | 36 | 44 | |
| *Constellation* . . . | 36 | 44 | Capt. Stewart |
| *Congress* . . . . . | 36 | 44 | Capt. Smith |
| *Boston* . . . . . . | 32 | | |
| *Essex* . . . . . . | 32 | | Capt. Porter |
| *Adams* . . . . . . | 32 | | |

### CORVETTES

| | | | |
|---|---|---|---|
| *John Adams* . . . | 26 | | Capt. Ludlow |

### SLOOPS OF WAR

| | | | |
|---|---|---|---|
| *Wasp* . . . . . . | 18 | 18 | Capt. Jones |
| *Hornet* . . . . . | 18 | 18 | Capt. Lawrence |

### BRIGS

| | | | |
|---|---|---|---|
| *Siren* . . . . . . | 16 | | Capt. Carroll |
| *Argus* . . . . . . | 16 | | Capt. Crane |
| *Oneida* . . . . . . | 16 | | Capt. Woolsey |

## SCHOONERS

| | Rated | Commanders |
|---|---|---|
| *Vixen* | 14 | Lieut. Gadsden |
| *Nautilus* | 14 | Lieut. Sinclair |
| *Enterprise* | 14 | Capt. Blakely |
| *Viper* | 10 | Capt. Bainbridge |

## BOMB-KETCHES

| | |
|---|---|
| *Vengeance* | *Ætna* |
| *Spitfire* | *Vesuvius* |

As we have stated before, the *Boston*, that was burned afterwards at Washington, never put to sea, and the *New York* was a worthless hulk.

The *Constitution*, the *United States*, and the *Constellation* were built in the year 1797, the *Constitution* at Boston, the *United States* at Philadelphia, and the *Constellation* at Baltimore. They had been built in the most complete manner, and it might be of interest to give some figures in connection with the construction of these vessels, thus forming an idea of how they compare with the tremendous and expensive fighting-machines of to-day. The first cost of the *Constitution* was $302,718. Her annual expenses when in commission were $100,000. Her pay-roll per month was in the neighborhood of $5000. There had been spent in repairs upon the *Constitution* from October 1st, 1802, to October 1st, 1811, the sum of $302,582—almost as much as her original cost, it is thus seen ; but upon the outbreak of the war only $5658 had to be spent upon her to fit her for sea. The first cost of a small vessel like the *Wasp*, carrying 18 guns, was $60,000; the annual expense in commission, $38,000.

Although the *Constitution* was in such good shape, the *Chesapeake* and the *Constellation* were not seaworthy, and required $120,000 apiece to be expended on them before they would be considered ready for service.

An American 44-gun frigate carried about 400 men. The pay appears ridiculously small, captains receiving but $100; masters-commandant, $75 a month; lieutenants' pay was raised from $40 to $60. Midshipmen drew $19, an ordinary seaman $10, and a private of marines but $6 a month.

A 44-gun frigate was about 142 feet long, 38 feet 8 inches in breadth, and drew from 17 to 23 feet of water, according to her loading. An 18-gun sloop of war was between 110 and 122 feet in length, and drew 15 feet of water.

At the time of the declaration of war the officers holding captains' commissions were: Alexander Murray, John Rodgers, James Barron (suspended), William Bainbridge, Hugh G. Campbell, Stephen Decatur, Thomas Tingey, Charles Stewart, Isaac Hull, Isaac Chauncey, John Shaw, John Smith—there was one vacancy. On the pay-rolls as masters-commandant we find David Porter, Samuel Evans, Jacob Jones, and James Lawrence.

It is hard to imagine nowadays the amount of bitterness, the extreme degree of hatred, that had grown up between America and Great Britain. Before the outbreak of hostilities, smarting under the defeats of '76 and the struggle of the following years, with few exceptions English officers burned to show their contempt for the service of the new country whose flag was being sent about the world. During the presence of the American fleets under Preble and Bainbridge in the Mediterranean, insults were frequently forced upon them by the English. An anecdote which brings in one of our nation's heroes will show plainly to what extent this feeling existed. From an American vessel of war anchored at Malta a number of the junior officers had obtained shore leave; among them was a tall, handsome lad, the brother of the commander of the *Philadelphia*. Orders had been given for the young gentlemen to mind their own affairs, to keep close together, and to pay no attention to the treatment they might receive from the officers of the English regiments or navy. Owing to the custom then holding, the man who had not fought a duel or killed a man in "honorable" meeting was an exception, even in our service. There was no punishment for duelling in either the army or navy, even if one should kill a member of his own mess, so there may be some excuse for the disobedience, or, better, disregard, of the order given to the midshipmen before they landed. There was an English officer at Malta, a celebrated duellist, who stated to a number of his friends, when he was informed that the American young gentlemen had landed, that he would "bag one of the Yankees before ten the next morning." He ran across them in the lobby of a playhouse, and, rudely jostling the tallest and apparently the oldest, he was surprised at having his pardon begged, as if the fault had been the other's. So he repeated his offence, and emphasized it by thrusting his elbow in "the Yankee's" face.

This was too much. The tall midshipman whipped out his card, the Englishman did likewise. A few words and it was all arranged. "At nine the next morning, on the beach below the fortress." As he turned, the middy saw one of his senior lieutenants standing near him. He knew that it would be difficult to get ashore in the morning, and he made up his mind that, as the chances were he would never return to his ship at all, he would not go back to her that night. But what was his dismay when the officer approached and ordered him and all of his party to repair on board their vessel. Of course the rest of the youngsters knew what had occurred, and they longed to see how their comrade would get out of the predicament. *He had to be on shore!* But as he sat in the stern-sheets the lieutenant, not so many years his senior, bent forward. "I shall go ashore with you at nine o'clock to-morrow, if you will allow me that honor," he said, quietly. Now this young officer was a hero with the lads in the steerage, and the middy's courage rose.

At nine o'clock the next morning he stood in a sheltered little stretch of beach with a pistol in his hand, and at the word "Fire!" he shot the English bully through the heart. The midshipman's name was Joseph Bainbridge, a brother of the Bainbridge of *Constitution* fame, and his second upon this occasion was Stephen Decatur.

This encounter was but one of many such that took place on foreign stations between American and English officers. The latter at last became more respectful of the Yankees' feelings, be it recorded.

The following series of articles is not intended as a history of the navy, but as a mere account of the most prominent actions in which the vessels of the regular service participated. Two affairs in which American privateers took part are introduced, but of a truth the doings of Yankee privateersmen would make a history in themselves.

It will be noticed that the names of several vessels occur frequently, and we can see how the *Constitution* won for herself the proudest title ever given to a ship—"Old Ironsides"—and how the victories at sea united the American nation as one great family in rejoicing or in grief. To this day there will be found songs and watchwords in the forecastles of our steel cruisers that were started at this glorious period. "Remember the *Essex!*" "Don't give up the ship!" "May we die on deck!" are sayings that have been handed down, and let us hope that they will live forever.

# I
# THE THREE-DAYS CHASE OF THE "CONSTITUTION"
[July 17th, 18th, 19th, 1812]

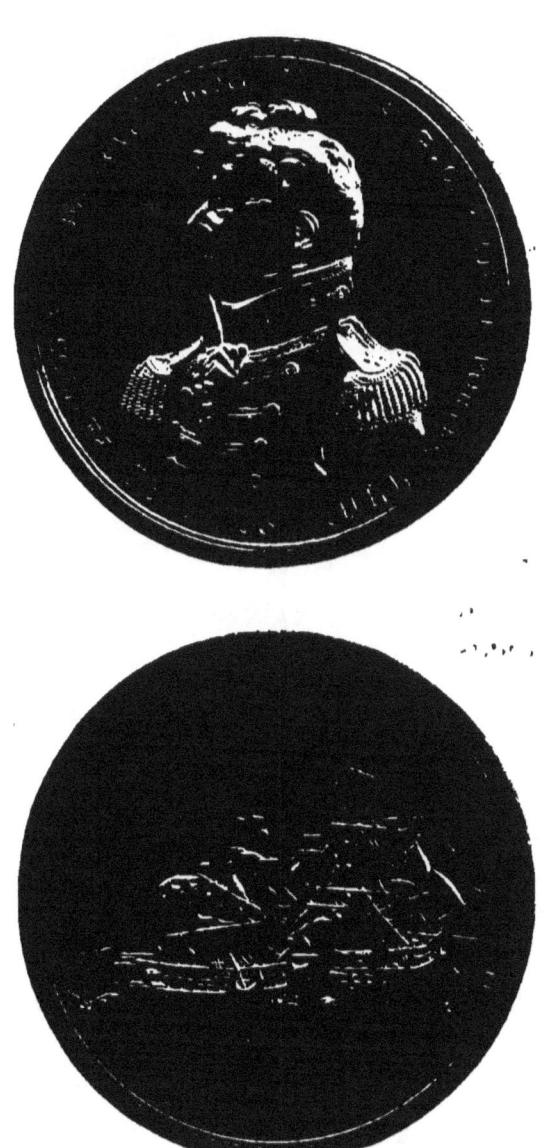

MEDAL PRESENTED BY CONGRESS TO
CAPTAIN ISAAC HULL.

IF during the naval war of 1812 any one man won laurels because he understood his ship, and thus triumphed over odds, that man was Captain Hull, and the ship was the old *Constitution*.

Returning from a mission to Europe during the uncertain, feverish days that preceded the declaration of war between England and America, Hull had drawn into the Chesapeake to outfit for a cruise. He had experienced a number of exciting moments in European waters, for everything was in a turmoil and every sail suspicious—armed vessels approached one another like dogs who show their fangs.

Although we were at peace, on more than one occasion Hull had called his men to quarters, fearing mischief. Once he did so in an English port, for he well remembered the affair of the *Leopard* and the *Chesapeake*.

At Annapolis he shipped a new crew, and on July 12th he sailed around the capes and made out to sea. Five days later, when out of sight of land, sailing with a light breeze from the northeast, four sail were discovered to the north, heading to the westward. An hour later a fifth sail was seen to the northward and eastward. Before sunset it could be declared positively that the strangers were vessels of war, and without doubt English. The wind was fair for the nearest one to close, but before she came within three miles the breeze that had brought her up died out, and after a calm that lasted but a few minutes the light wind came from the southward, giving the *Constitution* the weather-gage.

And now began a test of seamanship and sailing powers, the like of which has no equal in history for prolonged excitement. Captain Hull was almost alone in his opinion that the *Constitution* was a fast sailer. But it must be remembered, however, that a vessel's speed depends upon her handling, and with Isaac Hull on deck she had the best of it.

All through the night, which was not dark, signals and lights flashed from the vessels to leeward. The *Constitution*, it is claimed by the English, was taken for one of their own ships. She herself had shown the private signal of the day, thinking perhaps that the vessel near to hand might be an American.

Before daybreak three rockets arose from the ship astern of the *Constitution*, and at the same time she fired two guns. She was H. M. S. *Guerrière*, and, odd to relate, before long she was to strike her flag to the very frigate that was now so anxious to escape from her. Now, to the consternation of all, as daylight broadened, three sail were discovered on the starboard quarter and three more astern. Soon another one was spied to the westward. By nine o'clock, when the mists had lifted, the *Constitution* had to leeward and astern of her seven sail in sight —two frigates, a ship of the line, two smaller frigates, a brig, and a schooner. There was no doubt as to who they were, for in the light breeze the British colors tossed at their peaks. It was a squadron of Captain Sir Philip Vere Broke, and he would have given his right hand to have been able to lessen the distance between him and the chase. But, luckily for " Old Ironsides," all of the Englishmen were beyond gunshot. Hull hoisted out his boats ahead, and they began the weary work of towing; at the same time, stern-chasers were run out over the afterbulwarks and through the cabin windows. It fell dead calm, and before long all of the English vessels had begun to tow also. But the *Constitution* had the best position for this kind of work, as she could have smashed the boats of an approaching vessel, while her own were protected by her hull. One of the nearest frigates, the *Shannon*, soon opened fire, but her shot fell short, and she gave it up as useless. At this moment a brilliant idea occurred to Lieutenant Morris of the *Constitution*. It had often been the custom in our service to warp ships to their anchorage by means of kedge-anchors when in a narrow channel; by skilful handling they had sometimes maintained a speed of three knots an hour. Hull himself gives the credit for this idea to Lieutenant Charles Morris.

All the spare hawsers and rope that would stand the strain were spliced together, and a line almost a mile in length was towed ahead of the ship and a kedge-anchor dropped. At once the *Constitution* began to walk away from her pursuers — as she tripped one kedge she commenced to haul upon another. Now for the first time Hull displayed his colors and fired a gun; but it was not long before the British discovered the Yankee trick and were trying it themselves.

A slight breeze happily sprang up, which the *Constitution* caught first and forged ahead of the leading vessel, that had fifteen or sixteen boats towing away at her. Soon it fell calm again, and the towing and kedging were resumed. But the *Belvidera*, headed by a flotilla of rowboats, gained once more, and Hull sent overboard some twenty-four hundred gallons of water to lighten his vessel. A few shots were exchanged without result. But without ceasing the wearisome work went on, and never a grumble was heard, although the men had been on duty and hard at work twelve hours and more.

This was to be only the beginning of it. Now and then breezes would spring from the southward, and the tired sailors would seize the occasion to throw themselves on the deck and rest, often falling asleep leaning across the guns—the crews had never left their quarters.

From eleven o'clock in the evening until past midnight the breeze held strong enough to keep the *Constitution* in advance. Then it fell dead calm once more. Captain Hull decided to give his men

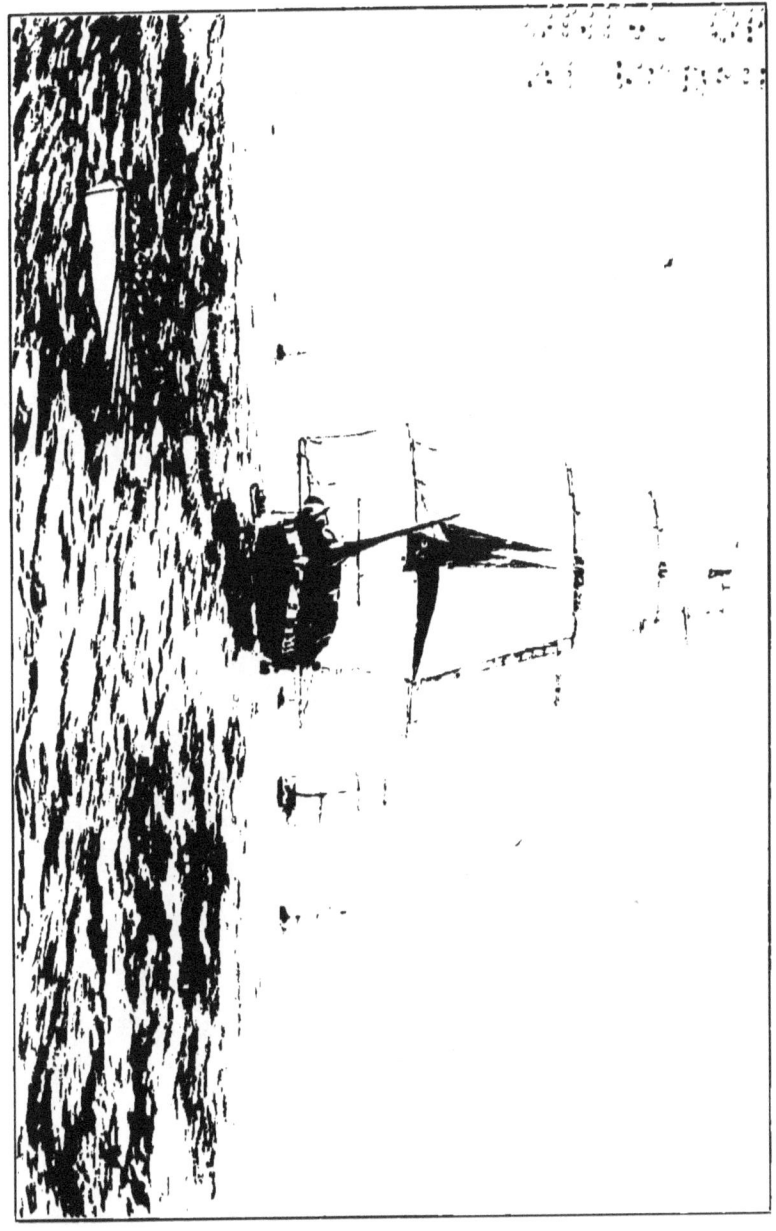

THE "CONSTITUTION" TOWING AND KEDGING

the much-needed respite; and, except for those aloft and the man at the wheel, they slept at their posts; but at 2 A.M. the boats were out again.

During this respite the *Guerrière* had gained, and was off the lee beam. It seemed as if it were impossible to avoid an action, and Hull had found that two of his heavy stern-chasers were almost worse than useless, as the blast of their discharge threatened to blow out the stern-quarters, owing to the overhanging of the wood-work and the shortness of the guns. The soundings had run from twenty-six to twenty-four fathoms, and now Hull was afraid of getting into deeper water, where kedging would be of no use.

At daybreak three of the enemy's frigates had crept up to within long gunshot on the lee quarter, and the *Guerrière* maintained her position on the beam. The *Africa*, the ship of the line, and the two smaller vessels had fallen far behind. Slowly but surely the *Belvidera* drew ahead of the *Guerrière*, and at last she was almost off the *Constitution's* bow when she tacked. Hull, to preserve his position and the advantage of being to windward, was obliged to follow suit. It must have been a wondrous sight at this moment to the unskilled eye; escape would have seemed impossible, for the American was apparently in the midst of the foe. Rapidly approaching her on another tack was the frigate *Æolus* within long range, but she and the *Constitution* passed one another without firing. The breeze freshening, Hull hoisted in his boats, and the weary rowers rested their strained arms.

All the English vessels rounded upon the same tack as the *Constitution*, and now the five frigates had out all their kites, and were masses of shining canvas from their trucks to the water's edge. Counting the *Constitution*, eleven sail were in sight, and soon a twelfth appeared to the windward. It was evident that she was an American merchantman, as she threw out her colors upon sighting the squadron. The Englishmen did not despatch a vessel to pursue her, but to encourage her to come down to them they all flew the stars and stripes. Hull straightway, as a warning, drew down his own flag and set the English ensign. This had the desired effect, and the merchantman hauled on the wind and made his best efforts to escape.

Hull had kept his sails wet with hose and bucket, in order to hold the wind, and by ten o'clock his crew had started cheering and laughing, for they were slowly drawing ahead; the *Belvidera* was directly in their wake, distant almost three miles. The other vessels were scattered to leeward, two frigates were on the lee quarter five miles away, and the *Africa*, holding the opposite tack, was hull down on the horizon. The latitude was made out at midday to be 38° 47′ north, and the longitude, by dead reckoning, 73° 57′ west.

The wind freshened in the early afternoon, and, the sails being trimmed and watched closely, Hull's claim that his old ship was a stepper, if put to it, was verified, for she gained two miles and more upon the pursuers. And now strategy was to come into play. Dark, angry-looking clouds and deeper shadows on the water to windward showed that a sudden squall was approaching. It was plain that rain was falling and would reach the American frigate first. The topmen were hurried aloft, the sheets and tacks and clew-lines manned, and the *Constitution* held on with all sails set, but with everything ready at the command to be let go. As the rush of wind and rain approached all the light canvas was furled, a reef taken in the mizzen-topsail, and the ship was brought under short sail, as if she expected to be laid on her beam ends. The English vessels astern observed this, and probably expected that a hard blow was going to follow, for they let go and hauled down as they were, without waiting for the wind to reach them. Some of them hove to and began to reef, and they scattered in different directions, as if for safety. But no sooner had the rain shrouded the *Constitution* than Hull sheeted home, hoisted his fore and main topgallant-sails, and, with the wind boiling the water all about him, he roared away over the sea at a gait of eleven knots.

For an hour the breeze held strong—blowing almost half a gale, in fact—and then it disappeared to leeward. A Yankee cheer broke out in which the officers joined, for the English fleet was far down the wind, and the *Africa* was barely visible. A few minutes' more sailing, and the leading frigates were hull below the horizon.

Still they held in chase throughout all the night, signalling each other now and then. At daybreak all fear was over; but the *Constitution* kept all sail, even after Broke's squadron gave up and hauled to the northward and eastward.

The small brig that had been counted in the fleet of the pursuers was the *Nautilus*, which had been captured by the English three or four days previously. She was the first vessel lost on either side during the war. She was renowned as having been the vessel commanded by the gallant Somers, who lost his life in the harbor of Tripoli.

Lieutenant Crane, who had command of her when taken by the English, and who saw the whole chase, speaks of the wonder and astonishment of the British officers at the handling of the *Constitution*. They expected to see Hull throw overboard his guns and anchors and stave his boats. This they did themselves in a measure, as they cut adrift many of their cutters—and spent some time afterwards in picking them up—by the same token. Nothing had been done to lighten the *Constitution* but to start the water-casks, as before mentioned.

So sure were the English of making a capture that Captain Broke had appointed a prize crew from his vessel, the *Shannon*, and had claimed the honor of sailing the *Constitution* into Halifax; but, as a contemporary states, " The gallant gentleman counted his chickens before they were hatched"—a saying trite but true.

To quote from the *Shannon's* log, under the entry of July 18th, will be of interest: " At dawn" (so it runs) "an American frigate within four miles of the squadron. Had a most fatiguing and anxious chase; both towing and kedging, as opportunity offered. American exchanged a few shots with *Belvidera*—carried near enemy by partial breeze. Cut our boats adrift, but all in vain; the *Constitution* sailed well and escaped."

It is recorded in English annals that there were some very sharp recriminations and explanations held in the *Shannon's* cabin. Perhaps Captain Hull would have enjoyed being present; but by this time he was headed northward. He ran into Boston harbor for water on the following Sunday.

Broke's squadron separated, hoping to find the *Constitution* on some future day and force her to action. In this desire Captain Dacres of the *Guerrière* was successful—so far as the finding was concerned; but the well-known result started American hearts to beating high and cast a gloom over the Parliament of England.

The ovations and praises bestowed upon the American commander upon his arrival at Boston induced him to insert the following card on the books of the Exchange Coffee-House:

" Captain Hull, finding that his friends in Boston are correctly informed of his situation when chased by the British squadron off New York, and that they are good enough to give him more credit for having escaped it than he ought to claim, takes this opportunity of requesting them to transfer their good wishes to Lieutenant Morris and the other brave officers, and the crew under his command, for their very great exertions and prompt attention to his orders while the enemy were in chase. Captain Hull has great pleasure in saying that, notwithstanding the length of the chase, and the officers and crew being deprived of sleep, and allowed but little refreshment during the time, not a murmur was heard to escape them."

It is rather a remarkable circumstance that the *Belvidera*, which was one of the vessels that in this long chase did her best to come up with the *Constitution*, had some months before declined the honor of engaging the *President*. For, on the 24th of June, Captain Rodgers had fired with his own hand one of the *President's* bowchasers at the *Belvidera*, and thus opened the war. After exchanging some shots, Captain Byron, of the *Belvidera*, decided that discretion was the better part, and, lightening his ship, managed to escape.

## II
## THE "CONSTITUTION" AND THE "GUERRIÈRE"
[August 19th, 1812]

THE history of the naval combats of our second war with Great Britain, the career of the frigate *Constitution*, and the deeds of our Yankee commodores will never be forgotten as long as we have a navy or continue to be a nation. England, it must be remembered, had held the seas for centuries. In no combat between single ships (where the forces engaged were anything like equal) had she lost a vessel. The French fleets, under orders of their own government, ran away from hers, and the Spanish captains had allowed their ships' timbers to rot for years in blockaded harbors. Nevertheless, this was the age of honor, of gallantry, of the stiff duelling code, when men bowed, passed compliments, and fought one another to the death with a parade of courtesy that has left trace to-day in the conduct of the intercourse between all naval powers. In the duels of the ships in the past that have stirred the naval world, America has records that are monuments to her seamen, and that must arouse the pride of every officer who sails in her great steel cruisers to-day.

Up to the affair of the *Constitution* and the *Guerrière*, in 1812, the British had not fairly tested in battle the seamanship or naval metal of the Americans. With the exceptions of the actions between the *Bonhomme Richard* and the *Serapis*, the *Ranger* and *Drake*, and the *Yarmouth* and *Randolph*, the war of '76 was a repelled invasion.

The twenty-four hours of the 19th of August, 1812, began with light breezes that freshened as the morning wore on. The *Constitution* was slipping southward through the long rolling seas.

A month before this date, under the command of Commodore Hull, she had made her wonderful escape from Broke's squadron after a chase of over sixty hours.

Her cruise since she had left Boston, two weeks before, had been uneventful. Vainly had she sought from Cape Sable to the region of Halifax, from Nova Scotia to the Gulf of St. Lawrence, for any sign of a foe worthy her metal. It was getting on towards two o'clock; her men had finished their mid-day meal, the afternoon drills had not begun, and an observation showed the ship to be in latitude 41° 40' and longitude 55° 48'. Suddenly "Sail ho!" from the mast-head stirred the groups on the forecastle, and caused the officer pacing the weather side of the quarter-deck to stop suddenly and raise his head.

"Where away?" he shouted to the voice far up above the booming sails.

Almost before he could get the answer the stranger's top-sails were visible from the lower rigging, into which the midshipmen and idlers had scrambled, and a few moments later they could be seen from the upper deck. The vessel was too far off to show her character, but bore E.S.E., a faint dot against the horizon.

Hull came immediately from his cabin. He was a large, fat man, whose excitable temperament was held in strong control. His eye gleamed when he saw the distant speck of white. Immediately the *Constitution's* course was altered, and with her light sails set she was running free, with kites all drawing, and the chase looming clearer and clearer each anxious minute of the time. At three o'clock it was plainly seen that she was a large ship, on the starboard tack, close-hauled on the wind, and under easy sail. In half an hour her ports could be descried through the glass, and loud murmurs of satisfaction ran through the ship's company. The officers smiled congratulations at one another, and Hull's broad face shone with his suppressed emotion. In the official account Hull speaks of the conduct of his crew before the fight in the following words: "It gives me great pleasure to say that from the smallest boy in the ship to the oldest seaman not a look of fear was seen. They went into action giving three cheers, and requesting to be laid close to the enemy." The *Constitution* gained on the stranger, who held her course, as if entirely oblivious of her pursuer's presence.

When within three miles, and to leeward, Hull shortened sail and cleared the decks; the drum beat to quarters, and the men sprang to their stations. No crew was ever better prepared to do battle for any cause or country. Although few of the men had been in action before, they had been drilled until they had the handling of the clumsy iron guns down to the point of excellence. They had been taught to fire on the falling of a sea, and to hull their opponent, if possible, at every shot. They loved and trusted their commander, were proud of their ship, and burned to avenge the wrongs to which many had been subjected, for the merchant service had furnished almost half their number.

As soon as Hull took in his sail the stranger backed her main-topsail yard, and slowly came up into the wind. Then it could be seen that *her* men were all at quarters also. Hull raised his flag. Immediately in response up went to every mast-head of the waiting ship the red cross of old England. It was growing late in the afternoon, the breeze had freshened, and the white-caps had begun to jump on every side. The crew of the *Constitution* broke into three ringing cheers as their grand old craft bore down upon the enemy. When almost within range the English let go her broadside, filled away, wore ship, and fired her other broadside on the other tack. The shot fell short, and the *Constitution* reserved her fire. For three-quarters of an hour the two yawed about and manœuvred, trying to rake and to avoid being raked in turn. Occasionally the *Constitution* fired a gun; her men were in a fever of impatience.

At six in the evening the enemy, seeing all attempts to outsail her antagonist were in vain, showed a brave indication of wishing to close and fight. Nearer the two approached, the American in silence.

"Shall I fire?" inquired Lieutenant Morris, Hull's second in command.

"Not yet," replied Hull, quietly.

The bows of the *Constitution* began to double the quarter of the enemy. The latter's shot began to start the sharp white splinters flying about the *Constitution's* decks.

"Shall I fire?" again asked Lieutenant Morris.

"Not yet, sir," was Hull's answer, spoken almost beneath his breath. Suddenly he bent forward. "Now, boys," he shouted, loudly, so that his voice rang above the enemy's shots and the roaring of the seas under the quarter, "pour it into them!" It was at this point, so the story goes, that Hull, crouching in his excitement, split his tight knee-breeches from waistband to buckle.

The *Constitution's* guns were double-shotted with round and grape. The broadside was as one single explosion, and the destruction was terrific. The enemy's decks were flooded, and the blood ran out of the scuppers—her cockpit filled with the wounded. For a few minutes, shrouded in smoke, they fought at the distance of a half pistol-shot, but in that short space of time the Englishman was literally torn to pieces in hull, spars, sails, and rigging.

As her mizzenmast gave way the Englishman brought up into the wind, and the *Constitution* forged slowly ahead, fired again, luffed short around the other's bows, and, owing to the heavy sea, fell foul of her antagonist, with her bowsprit across her larboard quarter. While in this position Hull's cabin was set on fire by the enemy's forward battery, and part of the crew were called away from the guns to extinguish the threatening blaze.

Now both sides tried to board. It was the old style of fighting for the British tars, and they bravely swarmed on deck at the call, "Boarders away!" and the shrill piping along the 'tween-decks. The Americans were preparing for the same attempt, and three of their officers who mounted the taffrail were shot by the muskets of the English. Brave Lieutenant Bush, of the marines, fell dead with a bullet in his brain.

The swaying and grinding of the huge ships against each other made boarding impossible, and it was at this anxious moment that the sails of the *Constitution* filled; she fell off and shot ahead. Hardly was she clear when the foremast of the enemy fell, carrying with it the wounded mainmast, and leaving the proud vessel of a few hours before a helpless wreck, " rolling like a log in the trough of the sea, entirely at the mercy of the billows."

It was now nearly seven o'clock. The sky had clouded over, the wind was freshening, and the sea was growing heavy. Hull drew off for repairs, rove new rigging, secured his masts, and, wearing ship, again approached, ready to pour in a final broadside. It was not needed. Before the *Constitution* could fire, the flag which had been flying at the stump of the enemy's mizzenmast was struck. The fight was over.

A boat was lowered from the *Constitution*, and Lieutenant Read, the third officer, rowing to the prize, inquired, with "Captain Hull's compliments," if she had struck her flag. He was answered by Captain Dacres—who must have possessed a sense of humor—that, for very obvious reasons, she certainly had done so.

To quote a few words from Hull's account of the affair—he says: "After informing that so fine a ship as the *Guerrière*, commanded by an able and experienced officer, had been totally dismasted and otherwise cut to pieces, so as to make her not worth towing into port, in the short space of thirty minutes (actual fighting time), you can have no doubt of the gallantry and good conduct of the officers and ship's company I have the honor to command."

In the *Constitution* seven were killed and seven wounded. In the *Guerrière*, fifteen killed, sixty-two wounded—including several officers and the captain, who was wounded slightly; twenty-four were missing.

The next day, owing to the reasons shown in Hull's report, the *Guerrière* was set on fire. At 3.15 in the afternoon she blew up; and this was the end of the ship whose commander had sent a personal message to Captain Hull some weeks before, requesting the "honor of a *tête-à-tête* at sea."

Isaac Hull, who had thus early endeared himself in the hearts of his countrymen, and set a high mark for American sailors to aim at, was born near the little town of Derby, not far from New Haven, Connecticut, in the year 1775. He was early taken with a desire for the sea, and at the age of twelve years he went on board a vessel that had been captured by his father from the British during the Revolution.

Although he entered the navy at the age of twenty-three, he had already made eighteen voyages to different parts of Europe and the West Indies, and had seen many adventures and thrilling moments.

During the administration of John Adams there occurred "that exceedingly toilsome but inglorious service" of getting rid of the French privateers who infested the West Indian seas. During this quasi war Hull was first lieutenant of the frigate *Constitution* under Commodore Talbot. In May, 1798, he had a chance to distinguish himself, and did not neglect the opportunity, although the upshot of it was tragic but bloodless.

It might not be out of place to relate the incident here. In the harbor Porto Plata, in the island of

St. Domingo, lay the *Sandwich*, a French letter-of-marque. Hull was sent by his superior, in one of the cutters, to reconnoitre the Frenchman. On the way he found a little American sloop that rejoiced in the name of *Sally*. Hull threw his party of seamen and marines on board of her, and hid them below the deck. Then the *Sally* was put into the harbor, and, as if by some awkwardness, ran afoul of the *Sandwich*, which, as a jocose writer remarks, "they devoured without the loss of a man." At the same time this rash proceeding was being carried on under the eyes (or, better, guns) of a Spanish battery, Lieutenant Carmick took some marines and, rowing ashore, spiked the guns. The *Sandwich* was captured at mid-day, and before the afternoon was over she weighed her anchor, beat out of the harbor, and joined the *Constitution*.

In the opinion of nautical judges this was the best bit of cutting-out work on record, for Hull's men were outnumbered three to one; and if he had not taken precautions, the battery could have blown him out of the water. But, alas and alack! all this daring and bravery went for worse than naught. Spain complained of the treatment she had received, and the United States government acknowledged that the capture was illegal, having taken place in a neutral port. The *Sandwich* was restored to her French owners, and, worst of all, every penny of the prize money due the *Constitution's* officers and men for this cruise went to pay the damages.

Before the war of 1812, Hull distinguished himself by his fearlessness and self-reliance during the Tripolitan war. The two occasions that gave him renown during our struggle with Great Britain have been recorded at length, and there is but to set down that, after the conclusion of the war with Great Britain, Commodore Hull was in command at the various stations in the Pacific and the Mediterranean, and departed this life on the 13th of February, 1843. Of him John Frost writes, in 1844, " He was a glorious old commodore, with a soul full of all noble aspirations for his country's honor—a splendid relic of a departed epoch of naval renown."

# III
## THE "WASP" AND THE "FROLIC"
[October 18th, 1812]

JACOB JONES, of the United States Navy, was a native of Kent County, in the State of Delaware. He rose rapidly through the various grades of the service, attracting notice by his steadfastness and attention to duty, and in 1811 he was transferred to the command of the *Wasp*, a tidy sloop of war then mounting eighteen 24-pound carronades. She was a fast sailer, given any wind or weather.

In the spring of 1812, Captain Jones was despatched to England with communications to our minister at the Court of St. James. After fulfilling his mission he immediately set sail for America. The declaration of war between England and this country took place while the *Wasp* was on the high seas on her returning voyage; but as soon as he had landed, the news greeted her commander, and he was eager to put to sea again.

Captain Jacob Jones knew his ship, he knew his crew, and he rejoiced in having about him a set of young officers devoted to the service. Their names were James Biddle, George W. Rogers, Benjamin W. Broth, Henry B. Rapp, and Lieutenants Knight and Claxton, and they were soon destined to win laurels and glory for their country.

The first short cruise yielded no adventure of importance, but on the 13th of October the *Wasp* left the Delaware and two days later encountered a heavy gale, during which her jib-boom was unfortunately carried away and two of her people lost overboard. For some hours she was thrown about like a shuttlecock, and all hands were called time and again to shorten sail. The night of the 17th the sky cleared and the stars shone brightly. To Captain Jones's surprise several sail were reported as being close at hand to the eastward. They were clearly seen through the night-glass to be large, and apparently armed. Jones stood straight for them, and gave orders to lay the same course that the strangers were then holding, and so they kept until dawn of the next day, which was a Sunday.

A heavy sea was running, and the *Wasp*, close-hauled, crept up to windward of the fleet that she had followed through the night. At the beginning of the early morning watch they were made out to be four large ships and two smaller vessels under a spread of canvas, all keeping close together.

But what was more interesting to the eager American crew was a sturdy sloop of war, a brig, that was edging up slowly into the wind, evidently guarding the six fleeing vessels to leeward—the sheep-dog of the flock.

The *Wasp*, having the weather-gage, swung off a point or so to lessen the distance.

As the stranger brig came nearer she heeled over

until her broadside could be counted with the eye, and her lower sails were seen to be wet with the spray that dashed up over her bows.

For some time the Americans had been aloft getting down the topgallant yards, and at eleven o'clock the stranger brig shortened sail and shook out the Spanish flag. But this did not deceive the wary Yankee captain for half an instant. No one but an American or an Englishman would carry sail in that fashion or bring his ship up to an enemy like that, and the *Wasp's* drummer beat to quarters.

Now for over thirty minutes the two vessels sailed on side by side, but constantly nearing. At last they were so close that the buttons of the officers' coats could be seen, the red coat of a marine showed, and all doubt on board the *Wasp* of the other being anything but English was dispelled in a flash. The matches had been smoking for a full quarter of an hour.

When within near pistol-shot Captain Jones hailed through his trumpet. Down came the colors of Spain and up went the cross of St. George. The distance was scarcely sixty yards, and as the flags exchanged the brig let go her broadside. A lucky incident occurred just then that probably saved many lives on board the *Wasp*. A sudden puff of wind heeled the enemy over as she fired, and her shot swept through the upper rigging and riddled the sails. Jones immediately replied with all his guns, that tore and hulled his antagonist with almost every shot; then, as fast as his crew could load and fire, he kept at it. Now and then the muzzles of his little broadside would sweep into the water; but those of the enemy, aimed high, were mangling his rigging and sweeping away braces, blocks, and running gear.

At the end of a hot five minutes there was a sharp crack aloft, and the main-topmast of the *Wasp* swayed and fell, bringing down the main-topsail yard across the fore-topsail braces and rendering the head-sails unmanageable. Three minutes more and away went the gaff at the jaws, and the mizzen-topgallant-sail fluttered to the deck like a huge wounded bird.

The American, slightly in advance, fell off her course and crossed her enemy's bows, firing and raking her at close range most fearfully. At once the fire of the Englishman slackened, and the *Wasp* drifted slowly back to her former position.

Both vessels were jumping so in the seaway that boarding would be attended by mutual danger. The enemy revived from the destructive broadside, fired a few more shots, and the last brace of the *Wasp* fell over her side, leaving the masts unsupported, and, badly wounded as they were, in a most critical condition.

"We must decide this matter at once," said Captain Jones, as he looked at the creaking spars, and he gave orders to wear ship. Slowly his vessel an-

THE "WASP" RAKING THE "FROLIC"

swered, and, paying off, the collision followed. With a grinding jar the *Wasp* rubbed along the Englishman's bow, and the jib-boom of the latter, extending clear across the deck immediately over the American commander's head, fouled in the mizzen-shrouds. It was not necessary to make her fast, and she lay so fair for raking that Jones gave orders for another broadside.

As the gunners of the *Wasp* threw out their rammers the ends touched the enemy's sides, and the muzzles of two 12-pounders went through the latter's bow-ports and swept the deck's length.

Jack Lange was an able American seaman who had once been impressed into the British service, and the excitement of the moment was too much for his feverish blood. Taking his cutlass in his teeth, he leaped atop a gun and laid hold of the enemy's nettings.

"Come out of that, sir! Wait for orders!" roared Captain Jones, who wished to fire again.

But if Jack Lange heard he did not hesitate, and, despite the command, hauled himself alone over the bows. Some of the men left their guns at this and picked up pikes and boarding-axes.

Lieutenant Biddle glanced at his commander, the latter nodded grimly, and with a spring the lieutenant gained the hammock cloth and reached up for the ropes overhead. The vessels lurched and one of his feet caught in a tangle, from which he vainly tried to free himself.

Little Midshipman Baker, who was too short to make a reach of it, thought he saw his chance, and, laying hold of Lieutenant Biddle's coat-tails in his eagerness, tried to swarm up his superior's legs. The result was, however, that both fell back on the rail, and came within an ace of pitching overboard into the sea. Jumping up quickly, Lieutenant Biddle took advantage of a heave of the *Wasp* and scrambled over the enemy's bowsprit on to the forecastle.

There stood Jack Lange, with his cutlass in his folded arms, gazing at a wondrous sight. Not a living soul was on the deck but a wounded man at the wheel and three officers huddled near the taffrail! But the colors were still whipping and snapping overhead, and, two or three more of the *Wasp's* boarders tumbling on board, the little party, headed by Biddle, made their way aft. Immediately the officers, two of whom were wounded, threw down their swords, and one of them leaned forward and hid his face in his hands.

The young lieutenant jumped into the rigging and hauled down the flag. It was almost beyond belief that such carnage and complete destruction could have taken place in a time so short. But a small proportion of the crew had escaped. The wounded and dying lay everywhere, the berth-deck was crowded, and there were not enough of the living to minister to their comrades. H. M. S. *Frolic* was a charnel-ship.

The *Wasp's* crew brought on board all their blankets, and the American surgeon's mate was soon busy attending to the wounded.

With great difficulty the two vessels were separated, for the *Frolic* had locked her antagonist, as it were, in a dying embrace; and no sooner were they clear than both of the prize's masts fell (one bringing down the other), covering the dead and wounded, and hampering all the efforts of Lieutenant Biddle and his crew to clear the decks.

All this time three great white topsails had been pushing up above the horizon, and soon it was made out that a large ship of some kind was bearing down, carrying all the canvas she safely could in the sharp blow.

Jones, thinking that it might be one of the convoy returning to seek the *Frolic*, called his tired crew to quarters, instructing Lieutenant Biddle to fit a jury rig and to make with his charge for some Southern port. It was not to be, however, and the gallant victory was to have a different termination.

The lookout on the foremast called down something that changed the complexion of matters entirely.

"A seventy-four carrying the English flag!" he shouted. That was all. The men at the *Wasp's* guns put out their matches. There was nothing to do but wait and be taken. Any resistance would be worse than foolish.

As the great battle-ship came bowling along she

passed so close that the faces could be seen looking through her three tiers of great open ports. She disdained to hail, fired one gun over the little *Wasp*, and swept on. Captain Jones hauled down his flag, and read the word *Poictiers* under the Britisher's galleries. In a minute or two the latter retook the *Frolic*, and, lowering her boats, placed prize crews on board both her and the Yankee sloop. After some repairing, she set sail and carried her captives to Bermuda.

As in all the separate engagements of the time, comparisons were made between the armaments and crews of the fighters, and the press of Great Britain and America began the customary argument. Probably the *Wasp* had a few more men, but to quote:

"The *Frolic* mounted sixteen 32-pound carronades, four 12-pounders on the main-deck and two 12-pound carronades. She was, therefore, superior to the *Wasp* by exactly four 12-pounders. The number of men on board, as stated by the officers of the *Frolic*, was 110. The number of seamen on the *Wasp* was 102. But it could not be ascertained whether in this 110 were included marines and officers, for the *Wasp* had, besides her 102 seamen, officers and marines, making the whole crew about 135. What, however, is decisive as to their comparative force is that the officers of the *Frolic* acknowledged that they had as many men as they knew what to do with, and, in fact, the *Wasp* could have spared fifteen men. . . . The exact number of killed and wounded on board the *Frolic* could not be determined, but from the observations of our officers and the declarations of those of the *Frolic* the number could not be less than about thirty killed, including two officers, and of the wounded between forty and fifty, the captain and lieutenant being of the number. The *Wasp* had five killed and five slightly wounded."

Captain Jones in his report speaks of the bravery of his officers, the gallantry of his adversary, Captain Whinyates, and makes little mention of himself. Upon his exchange and return to the United States he was received with every honor belonging to a victor, and the sum of $25,000 was voted by Congress to be divided as prize money among his crew. The *Wasp* soon flew the British flag, but was lost at sea. Strange to relate, this was also the fate of the second *Wasp* that was soon afloat in the American service, and that had a career which was surpassed by none of the smaller vessels of the day.

# IV
# THE "UNITED STATES" AND THE "MACEDONIAN"
[October 25th, 1812]

MEDAL PRESENTED BY CONGRESS TO
CAPTAIN STEPHEN DECATUR

> "Then quickly met our nation's eyes
> The noblest sight in nature—
> A first-rate frigate as a prize
> Brought home by brave Decatur."
> —*Old Song*.

EIGHTY-FOUR years ago, throughout the country, the name Decatur was toasted at every table, was sung from the forecastle to the drawing-room, from the way-side tavern to the stage of the city playhouse. To-day, written or spoken, it stands out like a watchword, reminiscent of the days of brave gallantry and daring enterprise at sea.

Those writers who have been tempted by their Americanism and pride to take up the navy as a field have repeated over and over again, more than likely, everything that could be said about Stephen Decatur.

On his father's side he was of French descent, as his name shows, his grandfather being a native of La Rochelle in France, and his grandmother an American lady from Rhode Island. He was named after his father, Stephen Decatur, who was born at Newport, but who had at an early age removed to Philadelphia, where he had married the beautiful Miss Pine.

On the establishment of an American navy he was appointed to the *Delaware*, sloop of war. This was after he had commanded one or two merchant vessels and had proved himself a seaman. When the frigate *Philadelphia* was built by subscriptions of loyal-hearted merchants, the command of her was tendered to the elder Decatur by the particular request of the subscribers. The value of inheritance could not be shown more strongly than by looking at the career of the son born to him on the 5th of January, 1779. At the time of the birth of Stephen Decatur, Jr., his parents were residing on the eastern shore of Maryland during the days the British were in possession of the town of Philadelphia. After the evacuation of that place they returned, and here their son was educated with the idea of making a sailor of him from the very first.

Young Decatur entered the navy in March, 1798, and joined the frigate *United States*, commanded by Commodore John Barry, who, by-the-way, was instrumental in securing the appointment for him. It was not long before he was promoted to be a lieutenant, and made a cruise on the Spanish Main on the brig *Norfolk* during the war against the French cruisers. Returning after the peace was concluded with France, he was ordered to the *Essex* as first lieutenant, and sailed with Commodore Dale's squadron to the Mediterranean. This trip he made twice more, for on the return of that squadron he was ordered to the *New York* under Commodore

Morris, who took the same station. After a short stay Decatur returned to the *United States*, and soon afterwards he was given his first command, the brig *Argus*, and with her proceeded to join Commodore Preble's squadron, and was transferred to the command of the schooner *Enterprise*, exchanging vessels with Lieutenant Isaac Hull. The story of the capture and blowing up of the frigate *Philadelphia*, which under Captain Bainbridge had run ashore and been taken by the Tripolitans, has been described times without number. There is not space to write about it here. It is a tale in itself. But after the success of Decatur's attempt, in which he overcame obstacles apparently insurmountable, the eyes of the country were turned upon him, and the great things that he afterwards accomplished were predicted.

Decatur was one of those men whose courage and lofty spirit make it impossible for them to remain spectators or mere directors of events in which they are interested. It was necessary for him to be in the midst of the fight, sword or pistol in hand, like a common seaman. The story of his duel with the Turkish commander in the harbor of Tripoli, where, with a sword broken at the hilt, he fought a hand-to-hand fight and emerged victorious, gives a little insight into his character. Upon his return to his country, after some short service he was appointed to the command of the *Chesapeake*, succeeding Commodore Barron, who had struck to the British frigate *Leopard* in 1807. It was here that the bad feeling between these officers that led to the tragic ending of Decatur's life began. As soon as the frigate *United States* was put in commission, Decatur was relieved of his command of the *Chesapeake* (which, to tell the truth, he did not much relish), and thus found himself, on the outbreak of the war with Great Britain, with plenty of opportunities before him to add to his laurels.

In October of the year 1812 the frigate *United States* was one of a small squadron that was cruising not far from the island of Madeira. On the twelfth day of the month she parted with the *President*, 44, and later with the 16-gun brig *Argus*, both of which had sailed with her from the port of Boston, all well officered, well manned, and eager to meet the enemy. Bearing away southward into the paths of the British West-Indiamen, Decatur, on the *United States*, hoped to intercept a rich prize or two, or, better, if possible, to fall in with one of His Majesty's vessels, which were constantly hovering in that neighborhood. Sharp lookouts were kept at the mast-head at all hours, and the crew were spoiling for action.

Sunday morning, the 25th, dawned bright and clear. There was a stiff breeze blowing, and the frigate was under easy canvas, steering a course southeast by east. An observation showed her to be in latitude 29°, longitude 29° 30' west. As soon as daylight was fairly broad, off to windward, close to the horizon, the lookout descried a sail, and in a few minutes it was discovered that the stranger was an English ship of war carrying all but her lighter canvas. Quickly the *United States* blossomed out from the topgallant yard to her main-course; and although the breeze was strong, studding-sails were set, and, tossing the heavy sea to left and right, she was soon hard upon the chase. The *United States* was a good sailer—all of our ships were in those days—and long before seven o'clock it was seen that she was overhauling the enemy rapidly. So great was the enthusiasm of her officers and men that the cheers they gave were borne by the wind to the Englishman before a single gun of the action had been fired. Through the glass it could be seen that the enemy were at quarters. At nine in the morning Decatur luffed a little, took in his lighter sails, and fired his gun-deck battery; but the balls fell short. Both vessels were now on the same tack, close on the wind, and Decatur found that it was impossible for the *United States* to gain the weather-gage.

Broadsides were exchanged as the distance was lessened, and for half an hour the commanders continued firing, doing no vital damage. Suddenly the enemy changed his course, squared his yards, and crossed Decatur's bows, letting drive his forward battery. Still the *United States* held on; and here the Englishman made a fatal error. It is given by some authorities that Captain John Carden, the commander of the *Macedonian*, supposed his opponent to be the *Essex*, which only mounted carronades; therefore he commenced action at long-range. It did not take long, however, to apprise him that he was out in his reckoning, for although the distance was so great that carronades and muskets were of no avail, almost every shot from the heavy metal of the American struck its mark, despite the pitching cross-sea. Finding it was too late to run, Captain Carden bravely bore down upon the *United States* to engage her at close quarters, as at the distance at which the action had commenced he was being literally chopped to pieces. It was reported that during the engagement, which then began in earnest, so incessant were the broadsides of the American vessel the Englishman supposed her to be on fire, and three or four times cheered in their turn as the news ran through the ship; but they were soon undeceived. The splendid gunnery of the Americans was apparent as the vessels neared. The rigging and spars of the *Macedonian* were riddled and cut, many of her guns were dismounted, and in a few minutes her mizzenmast went by the board. Pitching to and fro, shrouded in the smoke which blew towards her from the enemy's guns, the *United States* kept up her destructive fire. For an instant the smoke cleared away, and there hung the main-yard-arm of the English frigate in two pieces; her main-topmast was gone, her fore-topmast was tottering, and no colors were seen floating above her deck; her bowsprit was swaying to and fro, held only by the jib-forestay, and sailing was impossible. She ceased to gather headway, lurching and yawing to one side and the other helplessly.

Strange to say, the *United States* remained almost unhurt. Decatur ceased his fire as he saw the enemy's plight, furled his mizzen-topsail (the mizzen-topmast being badly wounded), drew away, tacked, and came under the lee of the English ship. She gave him a feeble broadside, and Decatur luffed again across her bows. As he did so, Carden, perceiving further resistance to be vain, hauled down his colors, which had again been hoisted on a spar at the stump of the mizzenmast.

Decatur, his face flushed with victory, hailed in person: "What ship is that?"

"His Majesty's frigate *Macedonian*, thirty-eight, John S. Carden," was the response.

Immediately a boat was lowered, and an officer was sent on board. In the two hours of the engagement she had suffered terribly. Not less than one hundred round-shot were counted in her hull, many of them between wind and water. She had nothing standing but her mainmast and fore-yard. Her boats were useless, with exception of one small quarter-boat; and out of the officers and crew, three hundred in number, thirty-six were killed and sixty-eight were wounded. The American loss was five killed and six wounded.

The *Macedonian* was but two years old, a fine

vessel of her class, rated thirty-eight, and carrying forty-nine guns—eighteen on her gun-deck, and thirty-two-pound carronades above. The *United States* was heavier and stronger, both in metal and men, it cannot be denied, having a crew of four hundred and seventy-eight. But, even taking into account the disparity in the weight of metal and the number of crew, the action proved conclusively that American-built ships and American seamen were to open the eyes of the world in conflicts on the sea.

Now comes the courtesy, the almost stilted politeness, that always seems as if prepared especially for dramatic effect before translation into history. As the brave Carden stepped upon the deck of the *United States* he proffered his sword to Decatur.

"No, sir," exclaimed the latter, doffing his cocked hat, "I cannot receive the sword of a man who has so bravely defended his ship; but," he added, smiling graciously, "I will receive your hand."

As an honored guest, Decatur led the vanquished to his cabin, where refreshments, to quote from another account of the affair, "were set out and partaken of in a friendly spirit by the two commanders."

Contrary to the opinion formed by the first inspection, Decatur found his prize capable of being refitted, and he determined to bring her to an American port. The *United States* was speedily repaired. In charge of Lieutenant Allen, who had made a jury-rigging for the *Macedonian*, turning her for the nonce into a bark, captor and captive set sail for the United States. On the 4th of December his prize entered the harbor of Newport, and it was upon this occasion that the old song was written from which the stanza at the head of this article is taken.

Nothing could be more dramatic than the way the victory was announced at Washington. Midshipman Hamilton, who was in the engagement with Decatur, and served with signal bravery, was sent with the captured flag of the *Macedonian* to present it to his father, Paul Hamilton, then Secretary of the Navy. He arrived in Washington on the evening of the 8th of December. A ball was in progress, and the Secretary of the Navy was present. The room was filled with beautiful women, with men in all the color and glory of gold lace, epaulets, and side-arms, when Hamilton entered. He carried the flag of the *Macedonian* wrapped about his shoulders. Instantly he was surrounded. The silk-stockinged dandies caught him up on their shoulders, and it is even on record that, strange to the customs of the times, dignity for once was cast aside, and a cheer rang through the ballroom. In the possession of the author is a letter (hitherto unpublished) written by Mrs. B. H. Latrobe, grandmother of the ex-Mayor of Baltimore, to Mrs. Juliana Miller. It gives such a graphic picture of the times that an extract from it cannot fail of interest. The letter is dated Washington, December 14th, and reads thus:

"The dulness of the city has, however, been removed in some degree by a splendid entertainment on board the frigate *Constella-*

*tion*. We were invited to be there at eleven, to pass the day. The vessel lay about half a mile from the shore, and two very elegant barges of twelve oars conveyed the company. This was the only unpleasant part of the amusement, for the day proved extremely cold, and a high wind was blowing. However, we all arrived safe about twelve, and the deck was closed in with flags, awnings, etc., and two stoves so effectually heated it as to make the temperature delightful. The dancing soon commenced, and continued till three, when the boatswain's whistle called us to a magnificent dinner below. The President and Mrs. Madison were seated at the end of a very long table; but I cannot tell you all the company, and can only say that the number was said to be five hundred. After dinner the dancing commenced again, and continued till about six in the evening, when the company broke up. On Tuesday a very splendid ball was given to the navy officers Hull, Morris, Stewart, etc. My husband could not be absent, as he holds an office in the Navy Department, and I was not sorry we went, as it is not likely I shall ever witness such another scene. At about five in the evening my husband came home, and informed me that we must immediately illuminate our house, as the account of a victory gained by Commodore Decatur had just arrived. My house in ten minutes was prepared for lighting up, and we prepared for the ball. The Avenue was very brilliant on our way to the Capitol Hill, and, the company assembling, the crowd was immense. Mrs. Madison was there, but not the President. The evening went on, with crowding as usual upon the toes and trains of those that did not dance, when, about ten o'clock, a loud huzza announced the arrival of young Archibald Hamilton, who had that moment appeared with the colors of the *Macedonian*. He was borne into the room by many officers. Good little Mrs. Hamilton, his mother, stood by me, and was so much agitated at the sight of her son that she must have fallen had I not stepped forward and offered her my arm. The young man sprang into her arms, his sisters threw their arms around him, and the scene was quite affecting. The colors were then held up by several gentlemen over the heads of Hull, Morris, and Stewart, and 'Hail, Columbia!' played, and there were huzzas until my head swayed.

"The aforesaid colors were then laid at the feet of Mrs. Madison. *O tempora! O mores!* This was rather overdoing the affair. I forgot to say that the flag of the *Guerrière* was festooned on one side of the room, and of some other vessel. Now, between ourselves, I think it wrong to exult so outrageously over our enemies. We may have reason to laugh on the other side of our mouths some of these days; and as the English are so much stronger than we are with their navy, there are ten chances to one that we are beaten. Therefore it is best to act moderately when we take a vessel, and I could not look at those colors with pleasure, the taking of which had made so many widows and orphans. In the fulness of my feelings, I exclaimed to a gentleman who stood near me, 'Good heavens! I would not touch that color for a thousand dollars!' He walked quickly away, I hearing another gentleman say, 'Is it possible, Mrs. Latrobe?' I looked around, and it was a good stanch Federalist from Rhode Island, Mr. Hunter, so that I shall escape hanging after so treasonable a speech."

Perhaps the circumstances were a valid excuse for the cheering; but this letter is a strange sidelight on some of the feeling of the times.

All through the country Decatur became the hero of the hour. With a record for intrepidity and gallantry behind him, gained by his actions during the war with Tripoli, handsome and young, he became the idol of the public. Congress, by a unanimous vote, gave him a gold medal. The legislatures of Massachusetts, New York, Maryland, Pennsylvania, and Virginia gave him thanks. The city of New York gave him the freedom of the city and a magnificent sword, and tendered to his crew a banquet at the City Hotel. Four hundred seamen sat down at the long tables, and the memory of that feast of rejoicing was long kept green in the service. As a picture of the day, a short account, taken from a contemporaneous history, *The War*, of the banquet given to Commodores Hull, Jones, and Decatur is of interest. The entertainment was given on the day after the freedom of the city was presented to Captain Hull. He and Decatur were present; Jones was absent. At five o'clock about five hundred guests sat down at the tables, De Witt Clinton, the mayor, presiding. "The room had the appearance of a marine palace," said an eye-witness. It was colonnaded around with masts of ships entwined with laurels, and having the national flags of the world. Every table had a ship in miniature with the American flag displayed. On the wall was a mainsail of a ship, and when the third toast, "Our Navy," was given, with three cheers, this sail was furled, revealing "an immense transparent painting of the three naval engagements in which Hull, Jones, and Decatur were respectively engaged." Too great to be spoiled, Decatur still remained the quiet, simple hero, before whose eyes were spelled two words—Country and Duty; the one he lived to serve, the other to fulfil. And, alas! he died a victim to that curious, strained sense of honor that kept men demanding explanations, and led them to shoot one another under God's sky, surrounded by their friends, in a duel to the death. He was killed by Commodore Barron at Bladensburg, Maryland, on March 22d, 1820. Commodore Bainbridge was Decatur's second, and he, with others, had made many ineffectual attempts to avert the unfortunate meeting.

# V
# THE "CONSTITUTION" AND THE "JAVA"
[December 29th, 1812]

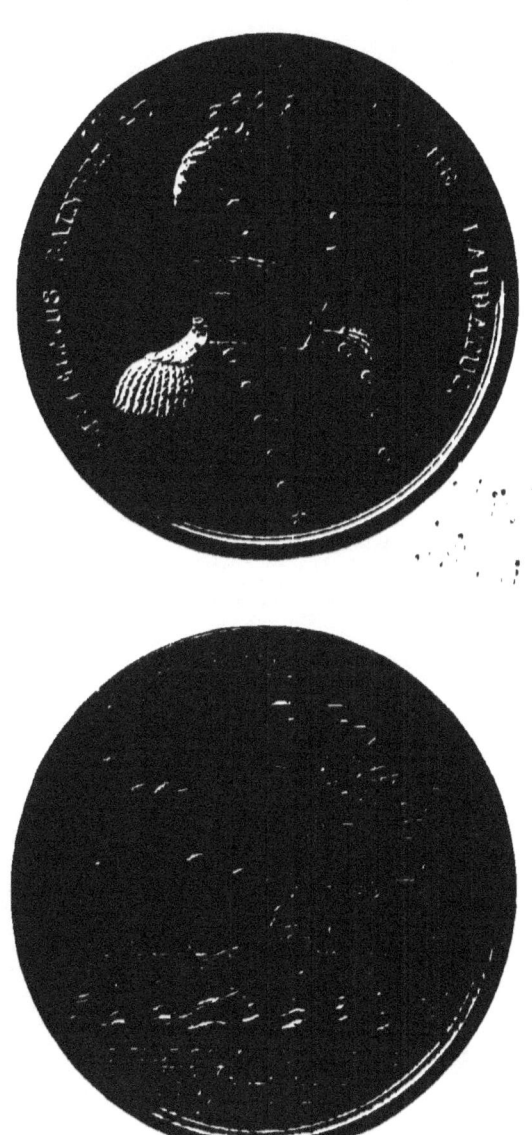

MEDAL PRESENTED BY CONGRESS TO
CAPTAIN WILLIAM BAINBRIDGE

WILLIAM BAINBRIDGE, commodore, was one of those commanders who were graduated from the merchant service to take high place in the navy of our country.

Owing to his own personal qualifications and character, he became renowned. Bainbridge was born at Princeton, New Jersey, May 7th, 1774. He was descended from ancestors of high standing, who had for several generations been residents of the State in which he was born, his father being a prominent physician, who, shortly after the birth of William, his fourth son, removed to New York. As a boy Bainbridge conceived a great love for the sea; and although under the care of his grandfather, John Taylor, he had been educated carefully for a mercantile pursuit, his desires and importunities were gratified, and at the age of fifteen he was placed on board a merchantman about to sail from the port of Philadelphia.

In order to test him, he was given the berth of a common sailor before the mast. Strong and agile, with his natural aptitude and born courage, it was not long before he began to show what he was made of. After his fourth voyage he was promoted to the rank of first mate on board a vessel trading between this country and Holland. During this voyage a mutiny arose which Bainbridge and the captain put down, although there were seven men against them. For this act, and in recognition of his skill as a navigator and practical seaman, he was given command of this same vessel at the early age of nineteen.

Bainbridge as a young man was not foolhardy, but he was of that stamp that brooked no interference with his rights, and allowed no insult to pass by unnoticed. While in command of the *Hope*, a little vessel of about one hundred and forty tons' burden, mounting four guns and having a crew of eleven men, he refused to stop at the hail of an English schooner; whereat the latter fired at him, and Bainbridge, probably to the Englishman's great astonishment, replied so briskly with his little broadside that the commander of the schooner actually surrendered, although his force consisted of eight guns and thirty men. Several were killed and wounded, and his vessel so much injured in the rigging and hull that he hailed Bainbridge, asking what the latter proposed doing with him. This was in the year 1796. There was no war between this country and England, and Bainbridge contented himself by calling the following message through his trumpet: "I have no use for you. Go about your business, and report to your masters if they want my ship they must either send a greater force or a more skilful commander."

A few days after this event, while on the homeward voyage, the *Hope* was stopped by a heavily armed British frigate, and one of her crew, an American, was taken out of her on the pretence of his being a Scotchman. Bainbridge offered to make oath to the contrary, but nevertheless the man was impressed. Within the same week Bainbridge fell in with an English brig much larger than his own ship, and, surprising her by rowing alongside with an armed boat's crew, he took from her one of the English sailors, leaving this message: "Captain —— may report that Captain William Bainbridge has taken one of His Majesty's subjects in retaliation for a seaman taken from the American ship *Hope* by Lieutenant Norton of the *Indefatigable* razee commanded by Sir Edward Pellew."

A contemporary adds: "The captured seaman received good wages and was discharged just as soon as he reached an American port, in no way dissatisfied with the service into which he had thus been forced."

Bainbridge's action in these small affairs attracted the notice of the Secretary of the Navy, and early in 1798 he was given the command of the *Retaliation*, a small vessel lately taken from the French by the elder Decatur. In the fall of the year the *Retaliation*, in company with the *Norfolk* and the *Montezuma*, two little vessels of about the same size, sailed for the West Indies, the squadron being under the command of Commodore Murray. Off the island of Guadeloupe, in the month of November, three sail were discovered to the eastward that were supposed to be English. At the same moment two other vessels were sighted to the westward. Commodore Murray sailed for the latter in company with the *Norfolk*, while Bainbridge was ordered to reconnoitre the three sails first sighted. Unfortunately they proved to be French, and, having the weather-gage, they closed with the *Retaliation* and ordered her to strike. As both of them were frigates, one being *L'Insurgent* and the other the *Volontier*, there was nothing for the young captain to do but to comply. The French commander, St. Laurent, declined to take Bainbridge's sword, gallantly observing that, as he had no opportunity to fight, he should prefer that he would retain it. At once both frigates set out in chase of the *Montezuma* and *Norfolk;* and *L'Insurgent*, outsailing the other Frenchman, was almost within firing distance of the two American ships when St. Laurent asked their force. The deception that Bainbridge practised, under the circumstances, was entirely pardonable; but in his reply he gave full swing to his imagination, and overstated the American armament by exactly doubling it, stating that the Americans were armed with 28-pounders and full of men. At once *L'Insurgent* was recalled from the chase, much to the chagrin of her captain, who stated that *les Américains* did not carry a gun heavier than six pounds, for he had been close enough to see them.

St. Laurent forgave Bainbridge the ruse, and treated him with great consideration.

After being in prison for some time, owing to negotiations, Bainbridge was sent to the United States in his own vessel, which was filled with liberated American prisoners.

Upon his return to his country he was promoted to the rank of master-commander, and put in command of the *Norfolk*, the ship he had saved. For over a year he cruised in the West Indies, meeting with many adventures, of which there is not space here to tell, and in 1800, at the age of twenty-six, he was given the highest rank then in our navy, that of captain, and appointed to the command of the *George Washington*, with the duty, much against his grain, before him, of carrying tribute to the Bey of Algiers. He fulfilled this mission; but there was not an end of it, as he was forced by circumstances to place his vessel at the disposal of the barbaric potentate, and to conduct a mission for him—no less than carrying an ambassador and his suite, numbering some two hundred persons, to Constantinople, the Bey wishing to conciliate the government of the Sublime Porte.

Despite his remonstrances, Bainbridge was compelled to do this, or the safety of every American in Algiers would have been in jeopardy, in addition to which the Bey declared he would immediately make war upon the United States. This disagreeable duty was performed, and the *George Washington* was the first vessel to fly the flag of the United States under the walls of Constantinople. The stars and stripes had never been seen there before; and as the name United States signified nothing to the governor of the Porte, Bainbridge had to explain that he came from the New World that Columbus had discovered.

On the 21st of January, 1801, Bainbridge was again in Algiers. He declined, however, to anchor in the harbor, as it was evident that the wily Bey was not to be trusted. Later in this year Bainbridge was transferred from the command of the *George Washington* to the *Essex*, which was one of a squadron of four vessels, consisting of the *President*, the *Philadelphia*, and the schooner *Enterprise*, under the command of Commodore Richard Dale, whose object was to protect American merchant ships from the depredation of the Tripolitan corsairs. Bainbridge was employed convoying merchantmen through the Strait of Gibraltar until the spring of 1802, when, his vessel being in need of repairs, he was ordered home. At once he was appointed to the command of the *Philadelphia*, to take up again the service he had left. On the 26th of August, not far from the strait, Bainbridge fell in with two suspicious sail—one a brig, and the other, apparently, one of the hated corsairs. He hailed them, and found that the brig was an American, and the other a Moorish vessel—the *Meshtoha*. Searching the latter, he found the officers and the crew of the brig under the hold, they having been captured nine days before. He retook the brig, placed her crew once more on board of her, and made a prize of the Tripolitan. This capture was a decided check to Moorish depredations. On the 21st of October, while Bainbridge was cruising off the harbor of Tripoli, sailing after one of the pirates, he unfortunately ran on a ledge of rock that was not down on the map which he possessed. All efforts to force the *Philadelphia* off the reef were unsuccessful, although everything was done to accomplish this; and after being subjected for five hours to the fire of numerous gunboats, a council of officers was called, and it was decided to surrender the ship as the only means of preserving the lives of her people. After this followed the long confinement, during which Bainbridge saw from his prison-cell the attempts of the American fleet under Preble to rescue him, and the destruction of the *Philadelphia* at last.

Shortly before the peace was made he was allowed to visit Preble's fleet, under pledge of his word of honor to return, although the Bashaw exacted that he should leave a hostage. He returned to his confinement, unable to effect conclusions satisfactory to the Turk and to Commodore Preble; but in 1805 the Tripolitans gave in, the prisoners were exchanged after their nineteen months of painful captivity, and Bainbridge returned to the United States, where he was greeted with the warmest sympathy and exonerated for the loss of the *Philadelphia* by a Court of Inquiry. After making successful cruises in various commands, Bainbridge, being in America at the time war was considered imminent between this country and England, hastened to Washington and appeared before the Cabinet, and, with Commodore Stewart, successfully urged the rehabilitation of our little navy, that, owing to the mistaken policy then in force, had been allowed to fall into sad decay. Delighted at the result, he returned to Boston, where he took command of the navy-yard at Charlestown, which position he held at the time of the declaration of war against Great Britain in 1812.

But, to quote from the *American Naval Biography*, by John Frost, "it is not to be supposed that one so adventurous as Bainbridge could be satisfied to remain on shore comparatively inactive when danger and glory were to be courted on the sea." Applying for the command of a frigate, the *Constellation*, 38, was placed at his service; but his arrangements were not completed when Captain Hull arrived in Boston harbor in the *Constitution*, after his victory over the *Guerrière*. Owing to some private affairs that demanded his immediate attention, Hull was obliged to resign his command, and Bainbridge, at his own request, was transferred to "Old Ironsides." The *Essex* and the *Hornet* also were placed under his orders, the former under command of Captain David Porter, and the latter under the brave Lawrence. On October 26th, 1812, the *Hornet* and the *Constitution* sailed out to sea, bound for the Cape Verd Islands. The *Essex*, then being in the Delaware, was ordered to join them there; but circumstances prevented her from carrying this out, although Porter did his best to find his superior officer and report.

Thus we find, in the latter part of December, 1812, the old frigate *Constitution* cruising in southern waters off the coast of Brazil. Her brave little consort, the *Hornet*, she had left blockading the *Bonne Citoyenne*, a British sloop of war, in the harbor of Bahia. Every day the *Hornet* dared the Englishman to leave her anchorage and meet her, broadside to broadside, in the open sea beyond the neutral limits and the protection of Brazilian guns. Writes Captain Lawrence of the Yankee sloop to Captain Green of the *Bonne Citoyenne:* "I pledge my honor that neither the *Constitution* nor any other American vessel shall interfere."

And, as if to emphasize this announcement, the *Constitution* spread her sails and sailed off to the southward, Bainbridge's last message to the watching Lawrence being, "May glory and success attend you!" But Captain Green was prudent; the English vessel kept to the harbor with her load of specie and her superior armament, and Bainbridge it was who won "the glory and success." Surely the *Constitution* was launched on a lucky day. About sixty hours after leaving the Island of San Salvador behind her, the *Constitution* was again clearing decks for action, and the men were cheering as they jumped to the guns. The following account is compiled from the *Constitution's* log and Commodore Bainbridge's diary:

It was the 29th of December; the vessel was in 13° S. latitude and 38° W. longitude, about ten leagues distant from the coast of Brazil. It was 9 A.M. when two strange sails were discovered on her weather bow. At 10 the strange sails were discovered to be ships. One of them stood in for the land; the other stood offshore towards the *Constitution*. At 10 Commodore Bainbridge tacked ship to the northward and westward, and stood for the sail approaching him. At 11 A.M. he tacked to the southward and eastward, hauling up the mainsail and taking in the royals. At 11.30 made the private signal for the day, which was not answered; then the commodore set mainsail and royals, to entice the strange sail off from the neutral ground, and separate her from the sail in company, which, however, was not necessary, as the other, with everything drawing, was making up the coast.

At 12 the American ensign and pendant were hoisted on board the *Constitution*. At fifteen minutes past 12 the strange sail hoisted an English ensign, and displayed a signal at her mainmast.

At a quarter-past one, the ship in sight proving to be an English frigate, and being sufficiently distant from land, Commodore Bainbridge ordered the mainsails and royals to be taken in, tacked ship, and stood for the enemy, who soon bore down with an intention of raking the *Constitution*, which the latter avoided by wearing. At 2 P.M. the British ship was within half a mile of the *Constitution*, and to windward. She now hauled down her colors, except a union-jack at the mizzenmast-head. This induced Commodore Bainbridge to order a gun to be fired ahead of her, to make her show her colors, This was succeeded by the whole of the *Constitution's* broadside. Immediately the enemy hoisted colors, and at once returned the fire. A general action now commenced with round and grape shot. But the British frigate kept at a much greater distance than the commodore wished. He, however, could not bring her to closer action without exposing his vessel to be several times raked. Both vessels for some time manœuvred to obtain a position that would enable them to rake or avoid being raked, and it was evident that the Englishman was cautious and well manned. In the early part of the engagement the wheel of the *Constitution* was shot away; but so well was she handled from below that her movements were hardly retarded. Commodore Bainbridge now determined to close with the British vessel, notwithstanding in so doing he should expose his ship to be several times raked. He ordered the fore and main sails to be set, and luffed up close to the enemy in such manner that his jib-boom got foul of the Englishman's mizzen-rigging. About 3 o'clock the head of the British vessel's bowsprit and jib-boom were shot away, and in the space of an hour her foremast went by the board; her main-topmast just above the cap, her gaff and spanker-boom were shot away, and her mainmast went nearly by the board.

About 4 o'clock, the fire of the British vessel being completely silenced, and her colors in the main-rigging being down, she was supposed to have struck. The courses of the *Constitution* were now hauled on board, to shoot ahead, in order to repair her rigging, which was very much cut. The British vessel was left in bad condition; but her flag was soon after discovered to be still flying. The *Constitution*, however, hove to, to repair some of her damages. About a quarter of an hour after, the mainmast of the British vessel went by the board. At a quarter of five or thereabouts the *Constitution* wore, and stood for the British vessel, and got close to her athwart her bows, in a very effectual position for raking, when she very prudently struck her flag. Had she suffered the broadside to rake her, her additional loss would have been extremely great, for she lay quite an unmanageable wreck upon the water.

After the British frigate struck, the *Constitution* wore, and reefed topsails. One of the only two remaining boats out of eight was then hoisted out, and Lieutenant Parker of the *Constitution* was sent to take possession of the frigate. She proved to be His Britannic Majesty's frigate *Java*, rating 38 but carrying 49 guns. She was manned by upwards of four hundred men, and was commanded by Captain Lambert, a very distinguished naval officer. He was mortally wounded. The action continued, from the time the firing commenced till the time it ceased, one hour and fifty-five minutes.

The *Java* was on fire and leaking; nothing could have saved her or the souls on board if the *Constitution* had been disabled.

The *Constitution* had 9 men killed and 25 wounded. The *Java* had 60 killed and 101 certainly wounded; but by a letter written on board the *Constitution* by one of the officers of the *Java*, and accidentally found, it is evident her loss must have been much greater. The unknown writer states it to have been 60 killed and 170 wounded.

The *Java* had her own full complement of men, and upwards of one hundred supernumeraries for British ships in the East Indies. Her force in number of men, at the commencement of the action, was probably much greater than the officers of the *Constitution* were enabled to ascertain. Her officers were extremely cautious in giving out the number of her crew, but by her quarter bill she had one man more stationed at each gun than the *Constitution*. The *Java* was an important ship. She had been fitted out in the most complete manner to carry Lieutenant-General Hislop and staff to Bombay, of which place he had been appointed governor, and several naval officers for different vessels in the East Indies. She had despatches for St. Helena, the Cape of Good Hope, and for every British establishment in the Indian and Chinese seas. She had in her hold copper for a 74 and for two brigs, building at Bombay.

The great distance from the United States and the disabled state of the *Java* precluded any attempt being made to bring her to a home port. The commodore therefore determined to burn her; she was set on fire, and the *Constitution* sailed away. Shortly after dark the British ship blew up. The prisoners were all landed at San Salvador and paroled, and, sad to tell, the commander of the *Java*, Captain Lambert, died soon after he was put on shore. The British officers paroled were: 1 lieutenant-general, 1 major, and 1 captain of land service; in the naval service, 1 post-captain, 1 master and commander, 5 lieutenants, 3 lieutenants of marines, 1 surgeon, 2 assistant surgeons, 1 purser, 15 midshipmen, 1 gunner, 1 boatswain, 1 master, 1 carpenter, and 2 captain's clerks; likewise, 323 petty officers, seamen, and marines—making altogether 361 men; besides 9 Portuguese seamen liberated, and 8 passengers, private characters, who were permitted to land without restraint.

Lieutenant Aylwin, of the *Constitution*, was severely wounded during the action. When the boarders were called to repel boarders, he mounted the quarter-deck hammock cloths, and, in the act of firing his pistol at the enemy, he received a ball through his shoulder. Notwithstanding the severity of his wound, he continued at his post until the enemy struck. A few days afterwards, when an engagement was expected with a ship, which afterwards proved to be the *Hornet*, he left his bed and repaired to quarters, though laboring under a considerable debility, and under the most excruciating pain. He died on the 28th of January, at sea. The following is the official account that Commodore Bainbridge made to the Secretary of the Navy. It is as concise and dramatic as all the reports of our naval heroes were in those days, and as he wrote Bainbridge was suffering from serious wounds and in danger of his life:

"I have the honor to inform you that on the 29th of December, at 2 P.M., in south latitude 13° 6', west longitude 38°, and about ten leagues distant from the coast of Brazil, I fell in with, and captured, His Britannic Majesty's frigate *Java*, of 49 guns, and upwards of four hundred men, commanded by Captain Lambert, a very distinguished officer. The action lasted one hour and fifty-five minutes, in which time the enemy was completely dismantled, not having a spar of any kind standing.

"The loss on board the *Constitution* was 9 killed and 25 wounded. The enemy had 60 killed and 101 wounded (among the latter, Captain Lambert, mortally), but, by the enclosed letter, written on board this ship by one of the officers of the *Java*, and accidentally found, it is evident that the enemy's wounded must have been much greater than as above stated, and who must have died of their wounds previous to their being removed. (The letter stated 60 killed and 170 wounded.) . . .

"Should I attempt to do justice, by representation, to the brave and good conduct of my officers and crew, I should fail in the attempt; therefore, suffice it to say that the whole of their conduct was such as to meet my highest encomiums. I beg leave to recommend the officers, particularly, to the notice of the government, as, also, the unfortunate seamen who were wounded, and the families of those brave men who fell in action.

"The great distance from our own coast, and the perfect wreck we made of the enemy's frigate, forbade every idea of attempting to take her to the United States. I had, therefore, no alternative but burning her, which I did on the 31st, after receiving all the prisoners and their baggage, which was very hard work, only having two boats left out of eight, and not one left on board the *Java*.

"On blowing up the frigate *Java* I proceeded to St. Salvador, where I landed all the prisoners on their parole, to return to England, and there remain until regularly exchanged, and not to serve in their professional capacities in any place or in any manner whatsoever against the United States of America until their exchange shall be effected."

Upon the return of Commodore Bainbridge to the United States he was everywhere received with the greatest joy. Congress voted $50,000 to him and his crew, and ordered a gold medal to be struck for him and silver ones for each of his officers. New York presented him with the freedom of the city, and many banquets were given in his honor.

A pathetic and dramatic incident occurred when the wounded Captain Lambert was being moved off the ship at San Salvador. He lay on the deck suffering intense pain, when Bainbridge, supported by two officers, approached. Bending down with great difficulty, he placed Captain Lambert's side-arms on the cot on which the latter lay, saying that the sword of so brave a man should never be taken from him; then the two wounded commanders grasped hands in mutual respect and admiration. The correspondence between Lieutenant-General Hislop and Commodore Bainbridge, after Lambert's death, shows plainly the lofty spirit that existed then between great-minded enemies.

# VI

## THE "COMET"—PRIVATEER

[January 14th, 1813]

DURING the war of 1812 the American privateers sent home to United States ports so many hundreds of British vessels that the printed list makes quite a showing by itself. The names of the prizes taken, their tonnage and value, were published in *Niles's Weekly Register*, of Baltimore, and each week during the progress of the war the number grew, until it seemed that the stock of *Laughing Lassies, Bouncing Besses, Arabellas, Lords* something-or-other, *Ladies* this or *Countesses* of that, must surely be exhausted. In they came to Baltimore, to New York, or Boston by the scores— brigs and barks, schooners and ships, sloops and transports. Some were next to worthless, some were valuable, and some were veritable floating mines of wealth; some were heavily armed and had been captured after fierce fighting; others had been picked up like ripe fruit and sent home under prizemasters. Each one, however, was stamped with the seal of her captor, who might be cruising anywhere from the China Sea to the English Channel. Eager for racing, chasing, or fighting, the American privateers were watching the highways of British commerce. What did they care for armed consorts or guard-ships? They could show a clean pair of heels to the fastest cruisers that carried the red cross of St. George, or turn to and fight out of all proportion to their appearance or size—and this latter was proved true in many well-recorded instances. They were the kestrels and the game-cocks of the sea. The names of some of them were familiar to every school-boy eighty-odd years ago—*Revenge, Atlas, Young Eagle, Montgomery, Teazer, Decatur, General Armstrong, Comet.* Here were some tight little craft that caused their powder-monkeys fairly to smell of prize-money on their return from each successful cruise.

All of these vessels were oversparred, overarmed, and overmanned. It was the privateersman's business to take risks, and many paid the penalty for rashness; but their fearlessness and impudence were often most astounding, and their self-reliance actually superb.

Up to the end of the first year of the war Maryland alone had sent out more than forty armed vessels, and, as a writer in the *Weekly Register* naïvely remarks, "not one up to date has been even in *danger* of being captured, though frequently chased by British vessels of war."

But to come to the affair of the *Comet*, privateer, of Baltimore. Her name had become familiar all along the Atlantic coast, her "winnings" were anchored in almost every harbor, and she could have the pick of the seamen lucky enough to be ashore at any place where she put in. Her 'tween-decks were crowded with extra crews and prize-masters to man her captures when she sailed out again.

The *Comet* was commanded by Captain Boyle, an intrepid sailor, and a man liked and trusted by his crew of 120 well-trained tars. She was as handy as a whip, and sailed like a cup-defender. She carried 6 guns in a broadside, a swivel, and a gun amidships.

It was on the 9th of January, 1813, that Captain Boyle spoke a Portuguese coasting-vessel which had just left the harbor of Pernambuco, Brazil, and learned that in the harbor were three English vessels loaded and ready to sail for Europe—one large armed ship and two armed brigs.

Upon hearing this welcome news Captain Boyle shortened sail, and tacked back and forth for five days, waiting and watching. On the 14th of the month his sharp lookout was rewarded by the sight of not three but four sail coming offshore before the wind. The *Comet* sheered away to the southward, and lay by, to give the strangers an opportunity of passing her. When they had done so, she put after them. It was quite late in the afternoon, a tremendous sea was running, and a freshening breeze lifted the *Comet* up the sides of the huge waves and raced her down into the hollows. She overhauled the other vessels as if they had been anchored. They kept close together, rising and then sinking hulls out of sight in the great seas. They evidently had no fear of the little vessel bearing down upon them, for they made no effort to spread their lighter sails. The *Comet* was under a press of canvas, and the water was roaring and tumbling every now and then over her forward rails.

At six o'clock, or thereabouts, the reason for the leisurely movements of the chase was discovered—one of the vessels was seen to be a large man-of-war brig. She was hanging back, evidently awaiting the American's approach. The speed of the *Comet* was not lessened, not a stitch was taken in, but quickly the guns were loaded with round shot and grape, and the decks were cleared for action. Then Captain Boyle hoisted the American flag. The other hoisted Portuguese colors. As the *Comet* sheered up close, the stranger hailed and requested the privilege of sending a boat on board, saying he wished to speak with the American captain on a matter of importance.

Accordingly, the *Comet* hove to, and her commander received the Portuguese officer a few minutes later at the companion-way. The conversation, in view of subsequent proceedings, must have been extremely interesting. The officer was a little taken aback when he saw the men standing stripped to the waist about the guns, the look of determination and the man-o'-war appearance everywhere. But he doffed his hat, and informed Captain Boyle sententiously that the vessel he had just left belonged to His Majesty of Portugal, that she carried twenty 32-pounders and a crew of 165 men.

Captain Boyle replied that he had admired her appearance greatly.

The Portuguese officer then went on to say that the three other vessels ahead were English, and were under the protection of the commander of his brig.

"By what right?" answered the captain of the *Comet*. "This is an American cruiser. We are on the high seas, the highway of all nations, and surely it belongs to America as much as to the King of Great Britain or the King of Portugal."

The officer upon this asked to see the *Comet's* authority from her government. This Captain Boyle courteously showed to him. After reading the papers carefully, the officer began to advise the American captain in a manner that provoked the following reply: "I told him," writes Boyle, in the log-book of the *Comet*, "that I was determined to exercise the authority I had, and capture those vessels if I could. He said that he should be sorry if anything disagreeable took place; that they were ordered to protect them, and should do so. I answered him that I should equally feel regret that anything disagreeable should occur; that if it did he would be the aggressor, as I did not intend to fire upon him first; that if he did attempt to oppose me or to fire upon me when trying to take those English vessels, we must try our respective strengths, as I was well prepared for such an event and should not shrink from it. He then informed me that those vessels were armed and very strong. I told him that I valued their strength but little, and would very soon put it to the test."

What a fine old fighter this Baltimore captain must have been! Here were four vessels, each of the three smaller ones as large as his own, and one nearly twice as large, against him; the Portuguese mounting twenty guns, the English ship fourteen, and the smaller brigs ten guns apiece. Fifty-four guns against fourteen. But the American was undaunted, and the Portuguese lieutenant rowed back to his ship.

Shortly afterwards the brig hailed again, asking Captain Boyle to lower his boat and come on board.

"It is growing too dark!" shouted Captain Boyle through his speaking-trumpet, and he squared his yards and made all sail for the nearest English vessel—the big ship.

So fast a sailer was the *Comet* and so quick in stays that she could shuttle back and forth through the little fleet in a manner that, to say the least, must have been confusing to the others. The moon was now coming out bright as the sun went down; but little of daylight was left.

The *Comet* came up handily with the English ship (the brigs were sailing close by), and Boyle ordered her to back her main-topsail or he would fire a broadside into her. So great was the headway of the privateer, however, that she shot past, and had to luff about the other's bows, Boyle again hailing, and saying he was coming down on the other side.

The man-of-war brig had crowded on all sail, and was hard after the American; but the latter now let drive her broadside at the ship and one of her smaller consorts, tacked quickly, and then found the man-of-war close alongside. The Portuguese, disregarding the policy of "minding one's own business," opened up her broadside upon the American. The *Comet* returned this with tremendous effect, and, tacking, again let go her starboard battery at the third Englishman, who was now closing in. Nothing but bad gunnery and good sailing must have saved the daring little vessel at this moment. But she loaded and fired, and the enemy appeared to be confused and frightened. The *Comet* stuck close to the English vessels, letting go whole broadsides into them at point-blank distance, and firing at the man-of-war whenever she came in range. The British vessels separated at last to give their "protector" a better chance, but it availed them very little. By the time the Portuguese was ready to fire the *Comet* had spun about on her heel and was out of danger. It was the clever boxer in a crowd of clumsy bumpkins. At eleven o'clock the big ship surrendered, being cut almost to pieces and quite unmanageable. It was broad moonlight; but the moon would soon go down, and in the ensuing darkness Captain Boyle feared the others might escape him. As soon as the ship hauled down her colors he gave the first brig a broadside that ripped her bulwarks and cut away her running-gear. Immediately down came her flag, and she surrendered also. She proved to be the *Bowes*, of Liverpool.

The sea was yet running very high, but a boat was manned and lowered away with a prize-crew, and made straight for the latest capture. When the heavily laden boat was a short distance from the *Comet*, around the bows of the captured ship came the man-of-war. She fired a broadside at the rowboat, and nearly swamped it there and then; half full of water, it returned to the *Comet*. Taking the boat's crew on board once more, the privateer headed for the Portuguese. Captain Boyle's blood was now up with a vengeance, and in the hot exchange that followed the bumptious foreigner had so much the worst of it that he withdrew from the engagement, and left the third English vessel to her fate. Like the others, the last hauled down her flag to save herself from further punishment. The situation was unusual. It was almost pitch-dark, and, heaving about to leeward, the three captured vessels were hardly discernible. The *Bowes* was taken possession of, she being the nearest, and the captain of the ship *George*, of Liverpool, reported that he could hardly keep his vessel afloat. The other brig, the *Gambier*, of Hull, was in much the same condition. Captain Boyle determined to stand by them both until daybreak.

As soon as it was light, it was seen that the little

fleet had drifted in towards land, the wind having changed during the early morning. The Portuguese had once more joined them, and made a feint of desiring to fight again. The *Comet* sailed to meet her; but the brig turned tail, signalled the *George* and the *Gambier* to make for shore, and followed as quickly as she could. Captain Boyle did not overtake them, and the three reached Pernambuco in safety—the ship in a sinking condition, the brig likewise, and the cockpit of the man-of-war, which was badly cut up below and aloft, filled with dead and wounded. The *Comet* and the *Bowes* reached the United States in safety, the former making several more important captures, and sailing through the entire English blockading squadron in the Chesapeake Bay to her wharf in the city of Baltimore.

# VII

# THE "HORNET" AND THE "PEACOCK"
[February 24th, 1813]

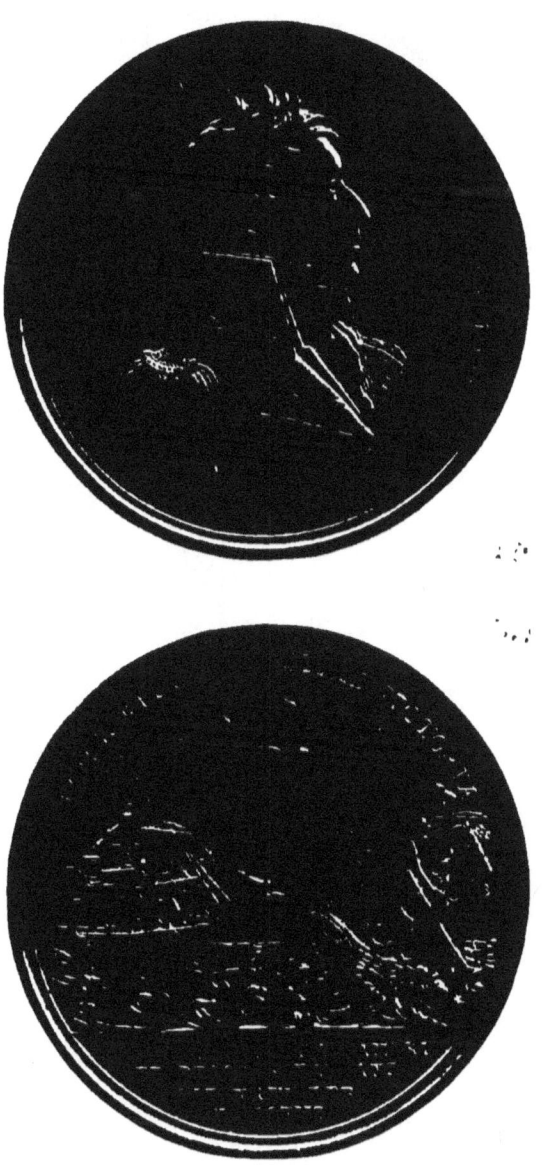

MEDAL PRESENTED BY CONGRESS TO
CAPTAIN JAMES LAWRENCE

AFTER Commodore Bainbridge sailed southward from Bahia on the cruise in which he fell in with and captured His Britannic Majesty's frigate *Java*, Captain Lawrence of the United States sloop *Hornet* had hoped to coax the *Bonne Citoyenne*, the English armed ship he was blockading, to leave the safe moorings which she kept so closely in the harbor of San Salvador. Captain Lawrence prayed each day that she might venture out and give his gunners a mark worthy of their skill. One morning, as the little *Hornet* was lifting and tugging at her anchor in the rough water at the entrance to the outer harbor, keeping a watchful eye on the spars of the *Bonne Citoyenne* and on those of another British packet of 12 guns that lay well inshore, a huge cloud of canvas came in sight to the eastward. Spar and sail she rose out of the horizon sky, until it was plainly seen that she was a line-of-battle ship flying the English flag. The *Montagu* (74) had heard the news of the *Bonne Citoyenne's* plight, word having been brought to her as she lay in the harbor of Rio Janeiro. Immediately she had set sail for San Salvador to raise the blockade. Reluctantly Captain Lawrence, on sight of her, got up his anchor and slipped into the harbor. He did not stay there long, however, and, after tacking about some time, escaped to sea that same night at nine o'clock. There were no ships of the line in the American navy at that time, and, perforce, the only thing left for any of our cruisers to do was to give those of the enemy the widest berth. So Lawrence, in the *Hornet*, shifted his cruising-grounds and went out into blue water. On the 4th of February, 1813, he captured the British brig *Resolution*, of 10 guns, and, not caring to man her, he took out $23,000 in specie and set her on fire. Then for over a week the *Hornet* cruised to and fro off the coast of Maranham without sighting a single sail. On the 22d of February Lawrence stood for Demerara, and on the 24th he discovered a brig off to leeward. At once he gave chase, but running into shallow water, and having no pilot, he had to haul offshore, much to his disgust, as the other vessel made her way in near the mouth of the Demerara River, and anchored close to a small fort about two and a half leagues from the outer bar, where the *Hornet* had been forced to come about. As the latter had done so, however, her lookout had discovered a vessel at anchor half-way in towards the shore. A peep through the glass showed her to be a brig of war with the English colors flying. Captain Lawrence determined to get at her; but to do this he had to beat to windward to avoid a wide shoal on which the waves were breaking furiously. At 3 P.M., as he had about made up his mind that the vessel at anchor and the *Hornet* were surely to try conclusions, Lawrence discovered another sail on his weather-quarter and edging down towards him.

In a few minutes over an hour the new-comer hoisted English colors also, and was seen to be a large man-o'-war brig. The *Hornet* cleared for action. As was usual in all naval actions when the wind was the sole motive power, both vessels manœuvred for a time, the *Hornet* trying to win the advantage of the weather-gage from her antagonist. But do his best Lawrence could not get it until another hour had passed; then finding that the *Hornet* was a better sailer than the English brig, he came about. The two vessels passed each other on different tacks at the distance of a few hundred feet—half pistol-shot.

Up to this time not a gun had been fired in the affair. But as they came abreast they exchanged broadsides, the Englishman going high, but the *Hornet's* round and grape playing havoc with the enemy's lower rigging. The brig held on for a few minutes, and then Lawrence discovered her to be in the act of wearing. He seized his opportunity, bore up, and receiving the starboard broadside, which did him little damage, he took a position close under the brig's starboard quarter. So well directed was the vicious fire that was now poured into the English vessel that in less than fifteen minutes down came her flag. No sooner had it reached the deck, however, when another crawled up in the fore-rigging. It was an ensign, union down; the brig was sinking. The sea was heavy, and before a boat could be lowered down came the Englishman's main-mast. Lieutenant Shubrick, who had been on the *Constitution* when she captured the *Guerrière* and the *Java*, put out in one of the *Hornet's* boats, and soon reached the captured vessel's side, and found that she was H.B.M. brig *Peacock*, 22 guns, commanded by Captain William Peake, who had been killed by the last broadside from the *Hornet*. There was not one moment to lose; six feet of water were in the hold, and the *Peacock's* decks were crowded with dead and wounded. She was settling fast. Her anchor was let go, and the *Hornet* coming up, let go hers also close alongside. Every endeavor was now made to save life; the men who a few minutes before had been fighting one another pulled on the same rope together and manned the same boats. The *Peacock's* guns were thrown overboard; such shot-holes as could be got at were plugged; but the water gained despite the furious men at the pumps and the bailing at the hatchways. The *Peacock* was doomed. The body of Captain Peake was carried into his cabin and covered with the flag he had died so bravely defending, to sink with her—"a shroud and sepulchre worthy so brave a sailor." All but some of the slightly wounded had been removed, and there remained but a boat-load more to

THE "PLUCKY" AND "HORNET" AT CLOSE QUARTERS

take off the lurching wreck, when she suddenly pitched forward and sank in five and a half fathoms, carrying down with her thirteen of her own crew and three American seamen—John Hart, Joseph Williams, and Hannibal Boyd. Fine old down-east names, mark you.

A boat belonging to the *Peacock* broke away with four of her crew in it before the vessel sank. They probably tried to make their escape to land. In writing about this little episode afterwards, Lawrence says, "I sincerely hope they reached the shore; but from the heavy sea running at the time, the shattered state of the boat, and the difficulty of landing on the coast, I am fearful they were lost." Captain Lawrence's treatment of his prisoners was such as uniformly characterized the officers of our navy, "who won by their magnanimity those whom they had conquered by their valor."

The loss on board the *Hornet*, outside of the three seamen drowned, was trifling—one man killed and three wounded, two by the explosion of a cartridge. The vessel received little or no damage. All the time that the action was being fought the other brig lay in full sight, about six miles off (she proved afterwards to have been *L'Espiègle*, of 16 guns), but she showed no desire to enter into the conflict. Thinking that she might wish to meet the *Hornet* later, Lawrence made every exertion to prepare his ship for a second action, and by nine o'clock a new set of sails was bent, wounded spars secured, boats stowed away, and the *Hornet* was ready to fight again. At 2 A.M. she got under way, and stood to the westward and northward under easy sail.

On mustering the next morning it was found that there were 277 souls on board, including the crew of the American brig *Hunter*, of Portland, Maine, captured by the *Peacock* a few days before. The latter was one of the finest vessels of her class in the English navy; she was broader by five inches than the *Hornet*, but not so long by four feet. Her tonnage must have been about the same. Her crew consisted of 130 men.

To quote from an account of the times which describes the return of the victorious *Hornet* to the United States: "The officers of the *Peacock* were so affected by the treatment they received from Captain Lawrence that on their arrival at New York they made grateful acknowledgment of it in the papers. To use their own phrase, 'They ceased to consider themselves prisoners.' Nor must we omit to mention a circumstance highly to the honor of the brave tars of the *Hornet*. Finding that the crew of the *Peacock* had lost all their clothing by the sudden sinking of their vessel, they made a subscription, and from their own chest supplied each man with two shirts and a blue jacket and trousers. Such may rough sailors be made when they have before them the example of high-minded men."

It was not long before poor Lawrence was to be

borne on the shoulders of his enemies and laid to rest, with all honors, in a foreign soil, a last return of the courtesy he had extended to all those whom the fortunes of war had placed under his care and keeping.

# VIII
## THE "CHESAPEAKE" AND THE "SHANNON"
[June 1st, 1813]

> "Let shouts of victory for laurels won
> Give place to grief for Lawrence, Valor's son.
> The warrior who was e'er his country's pride
> Has for that country bravely, nobly died."
>
> —From "*An Elegy in Remembrance of James Lawrence, Esquire,*" *published in June, 1813.*

NEW JERSEY claims the honor of being the birthplace of Captain James Lawrence, at one time the idol of the naval service. Captain Lawrence was born at Burlington, being the youngest son of John Lawrence, Esq. Although at the age of twelve he manifested a desire to become a sailor, his wish was not gratified until five years later, when, abandoning the study of law, he took up that of navigation, and received a warrant as midshipman on the 4th of September, 1798.

He made one voyage on the ship *Ganges*, under Captain Tingey, and after two years of cruising in various vessels he was made an acting lieutenant on board the frigate *Adams*, where he continued until the reduction of the naval force began, and then, his appointment not being confirmed, he once more found himself a midshipman.

Lawrence, like many a good officer, appeared to be continually at loggerheads with the department at Washington. He objected to this first reduction, and in 1801 his objection was sustained, and he sailed to the Mediterranean as first lieutenant of the schooner *Enterprise* in 1803. All through the war with Tripoli he conducted himself with such bravery as to bring commendation from all his superiors. As an example of his spirit and fearlessness an incident is well worth quoting. After he had returned with Commodore Preble he was not allowed to rest long in idleness; again he was sent to the Mediterranean, for what reason it would be hard to state; he was hastened away in command of one of the foolishly constructed gunboats that did not even rejoice in the dignity of possessing a name, being merely known on the register as " No. 6." None of these vessels was qualified to take to the sea. They were built on the model of great rowboats, and wallowed and tossed and pitched, and behaved in every way that a vessel ought not to when under sail. The one big gun they carried amidships on deck rendered them top-heavy, and, as some one wrote at the time, "the leeway they gathered discounted the log." But Lawrence grimly accepted the duty assigned to him, and set out at once. A few months afterwards one of his brother officers wrote in a letter to a relation in the army, saying, " Lawrence has told me that when he went on board the gunboat he had not the faintest idea that he would ever arrive out to the Mediterranean in her, or indeed arrive anywhere else. He also told me that on the coast of Europe he met an English frigate, the captain of which would not at first believe that he had crossed the Atlantic in such a vessel."

But he crossed safely, however, and cruised about in his cockle-shell for some sixteen months. Immediately after his return Lawrence was made first lieutenant of the frigate *Constitution*; then transferred to the schooner *Vixen*, of which he was given the command; whence he went to the brig *Argus*, and at last to the sloop *Hornet*. Twice he was sent to Europe in the latter with despatches to our ministers. Upon the outbreak of the war Lawrence was yet in command of the *Hornet*, which was one of the squadron of five sail that set out under Commodore Rodgers in the unsuccessful attempt to intercept the Jamaica fleet.

Much upset in his mind by the promotion of a junior officer over his head, only Lawrence's patriotism and loyalty prevented him from resigning from the service. The Senate restored him to his proper number on the list, however, and he sailed with Commodore Bainbridge in the cruise to the south, from which he returned soon after the capture of the *Peacock*.

In all history it is customary to count the incidents of unsuccessful but heroic resistance to the honor and glory of the nation. The historians of Great Britain in all their works rightly take this stand in detailing the actions between their vessels and those of the little navy of the United States.

There is on record in our annals the story of an unsuccessful engagement that cannot but reflect credit on our naval officers and our flag.

Jack Tars are more superstitious than any other class of men. They fear Friday, and are on the constant lookout for omens and portents. Give a ship an unlucky name and it counts against her in securing a good crew. The *Chesapeake* was an unlucky vessel. On the 22d of June, 1807, manned by a green crew under the command of Commodore Barron, she had left Hampton Roads. This was during the time that England was employing her assumed " Right of Search," that led to the struggle five years later.

Taken at a disadvantage, she was humiliated by being compelled to lower her flag to H. M. S. *Leopard*, after the latter had poured in several destructive broadsides without return. The *Chesapeake* had three men killed and eighteen wounded, and her commander was forced to submit to the kidnapping of four alleged deserters from his crew. The vessel had proved herself a slow sailer, and had accomplished nothing in her cruises. In March, 1813, she was lying in Boston Harbor, her complement of men not filled and her armament incomplete.

Captain Lawrence, fearing that he might be appointed to her, applied for the command of the *Constitution*.

High-spirited and sensitive, he had taken offence

THE "CHESAPEAKE" LEAVING THE HARBOR

UNIV. OF
CALIFORNIA

at the manner in which his request was received. The Secretary of the Navy entailed the condition that if neither Captain Porter nor Captain Evans applied for the command of "Old Ironsides," Lawrence could have her. Objecting to this treatment, he was given the appointment unconditionally; but the next day, to his chagrin, he received a recall of the order, and, after some vexations, counter-instructions to take command of the *Chesapeake*, then lying in Boston Roads. Lawrence was prejudiced against this ship, and disgruntled at his peculiar treatment; but to his respectful remonstrances the Secretary of the Navy vouchsafed no reply, and the gallant officer pocketed his pride and went on board his unfortunate command.

British vessels of war were a common sight from any hill along the New England coast. Outfitting at Halifax, they hovered about, and were in constant communication with one another, the smaller vessels seldom straying far from their towering guard-ships.

While Lawrence was endeavoring to teach the green crew of the *Chesapeake* something of discipline and man-of-war customs, a strange sail boldly made in to the entrance of Boston Roads.

She tacked about, flying signals of defiance. It was the *Shannon* (38), a prime vessel, magnificently equipped for the express purpose of meeting a Yankee frigate. She had an unusually numerous crew of picked men, thoroughly disciplined and well officered. She was commanded by Captain Broke, a fearless and able officer, one of the best in the service of Great Britain—a man who feared no danger, and fought with desire to gain reputation and glory. He had dismissed the *Tenedos*, line-of-battle ship, and wished to fight alone.

In Low's *Great Battles of the British Navy* the author speaks of Captain Broke sending a formal challenge to the captain of the *Chesapeake* to come out and meet "ship to ship, to try the fortunes of our respective flags." The English writer adds that "the redoubtable Captain Lawrence was not backward in accepting the challenge."

This challenge, a model of the stilted courtesy and frank gallantry of the day, was never received by the American commander, despite the statement. It might have made some difference, for it told the number of men, guns, and armament.

To Captain Broke's honor be it said that he sought no favor and he had no fear. An American publication speaks in the following words : " It is to be deeply regretted that Captain Lawrence did not receive this gallant challenge, as it would have given him time to put his ship in proper order, and spared him the necessity of hurrying out in his unprepared condition to so formidable and momentous an encounter."

The English exploited in verse and song the victory they had gained. A series of paintings and engravings representing different phases of the engagement was designed by Captain R. H. King, R.N., and painted by Schetky, and dedicated to Captain Sir Philip Bowes Vere Broke, Bart., R.N., K.C.B. The King, on hearing the news of the capture, is reported to have clapped his hands.

That Lawrence fought the action contrary to his own judgment, and was not sanguine of victory, is shown by a letter in his own hand, written on board the *Chesapeake*, and sent off by the pilot; for the American vessel, as she left the harbor, was surrounded by a fleet of small craft, which came out to see the action. This letter is addressed, " James Cox, Esq., Merchant, New York."

The following is a copy of the letter, the original of which is now in the possession of the author:

"*June 1st.*

" DEAR JAMES,—By the enclosed you will perceive that Bainbridge and myself have had a serious difference. It is in a measure, however, done away, in consequence of an explanation had last evening. You will pay him one and one-half twentieths of my prize-money, and demand the same resulting from the capture of the *Java*. . . . An English frigate is close in with the light-house, and we are now clearing ship for action.

" Should I be so unfortunate as to be taken off, I leave my wife and children to your care, and feel confident that you will behave to them the same as if they were your own. Remember me affectionately to our good mother, and believe me,

" Sincerely yours,

" JAMES LAWRENCE.

" P. S.—10 A.M. The frigate is plain in sight from our decks, and we are now getting under way."

Trouble soon came; the crew, that had never

sailed under Lawrence before, acted in a listless, half-hearted manner. A villanous boatswain's mate, a Portuguese, showed signs of mutinous conduct; for immediately after the *Chesapeake* was under way, and Lawrence had addressed a few words to the crew assembled in the waist, this scoundrel replied in an insolent manner, complaining that he had not received prize-money which had been due, he claimed, for some time past. It was impossible, in view of the fact that he was entirely unacquainted with the characters of his crew, for Captain Lawrence to notice this conduct in the manner it deserved. He had had no time to gain their affections or obtain influence through his personality.

Imagine the scene! With the enemy waiting in the offing, the disaffected ones were taken to the cabin and there paid the money that they claimed was owing them. As Lawrence looked about, he longed for the Yankee tars that had served under him in the *Hornet* and that he had hoped to command in the *Constitution*. His heart must have failed him.

Up went the flag. The English had learned to read without the glass, " Free Trade and Sailors' Rights," the motto painted on it.

As the *Chesapeake* approached, the English vessel hauled off shore.

It was a beautiful summer day. The water was rippled, and there was little or no swell. It was a day for target practice. The small craft either held back or had been left behind as the two combatants, sailing in silence, drew away from shore.

At 4 P.M. the *Chesapeake* fired a gun. The *Shannon* braced back her main-topsail and hove to. The smoke from the first shot had cleared away, and the vessels manœuvred for some minutes to gain the advantage.

Lawrence must have seen that it would have been better had he listened to the counsels of Bainbridge and others, who had advised him not to seek a meeting just at that time. It was evident that the *Shannon* was the better sailer. Several times the newly rove running-gear of the *Chesapeake* jammed in the blocks. Her crew were confused, and the men did not know their numbers at the guns. All exertions were made, however; but, after having been for some time within pistol-shot, broadsides were fired with tremendous execution. The first broadside that the *Chesapeake* received was a catastrophe in itself; the double-shotted guns of the enemy tore great breaks in her bulwarks, and officers who had occupied positions of great danger fell in every part of the ship. The first shot killed Mr. White, the sailing-master. The fourth lieutenant, Mr. Ballard, received a mortal wound; and at this same moment Captain Lawrence was shot through the leg by a musket-ball from the *Shannon's* tops. He made no outcry, but, leaning against the companion-way for support, continued to give his orders in a cool, firm voice. The ships were now so close that the powder smoke blackened their white streaks, and three broadsides were exchanged in quick succession that were frightful in their results.

The English had placed expert riflemen in their tops, and three men were shot successively from the *Chesapeake's* wheel. The American ship fell off from her proper course, and the *Shannon* veering close, her after-port was caught by the *Chesapeake's* anchor. The ill-luck of the latter vessel had followed her. For some time she could not bring a gun to bear, while the Englishman from his foremost guns raked her upper decks, killing and wounding the greater portion of the men there.

It had been for a long time a superstition with our cousins across the water that naught could resist the onslaught of an English boarding party. An exception, however, has been made in favor of the "damned Yankees" by a well-known English writer.

Seeing that the spar-deck of the *Chesapeake* was devoid of defenders, a party of the *Shannon's* men took advantage of a favorable chance, and, without waiting for orders, jumped on the American's deck. Captain Lawrence, still leaning heavily against the rail, and weak from loss of blood, had scarcely time to call his boarders to repel the attack when he received a second wound, from a bullet, in the abdomen. He fell into the arms of Lieutenant Cox, who commanded the second division, and was hurrying up from below. At this moment Captain Broke, of the *Shannon*, bravely headed a second boarding party, and sprang over the railing of the *Chesapeake*. Lawrence saw the danger as he struggled, with Cox's help, to rise from the deck.

"Don't give up the ship! don't give up the ship!" he said, and repeated it over and over as they carried him down the companion-way.

A hand-to-hand struggle now ensued. The only American officer remaining on the upper deck was Lieutenant Ludlow. He was so weakened and disabled by numerous wounds that he was incapable of personal resistance, and the small number of British succeeded in obtaining possession before those from below could swarm up to the defence.

An account gathered from an officer after the surrender speaks as follows:

"We were greatly embarrassed in consequence of being unacquainted with our crew. In one instance, in particular, Lieutenant Cox joined a party of the enemy through mistake, and was made sensible of his error by their slashing at him with their cutlasses."

Lawrence, lying below in the wardroom, suffering agony, heard the firing cease, and, having no officer near him, he ordered the surgeon who was attending his wound to hasten on deck and tell his followers to fight on to the last, and never strike the colors, adding:

"They shall wave while I live."

But nothing could be done. A ship without a

captain is a man without a soul. The fate of battle was decided. It was mere waste of life to continue, and Lieutenant Ludlow gave up the *Chesapeake*.

There was the utmost confusion during the latter part of the battle, but accounts differ in regard to the details. A hot-headed boy fired at an English sentry placed at a gangway, and started an action that resulted in Lieutenant Ludlow receiving a cutlass wound in the head which fractured his skull and proved fatal. An English authority, in speaking of the hauling down of the stars and stripes, recalls that Lieutenant Wall, one of their own officers, was killed, and four or five men fell, from a volley delivered by their own people from the tops of the *Shannon*, "for in the hurry and excitement the Yankee flag was hoisted uppermost."

Thus terminated one of the most remarkable combats on naval record. The action had lasted over a quarter of an hour. There is little use in surmising what might have occurred had not the ships run foul of each other.

The *Chesapeake* had received little injury to affect her safety, while the *Shannon* had several shots between wind and water, and could not have sustained an action at gunshot distance for any great length of time.

The two ships presented terrible spectacles, says a witness. "Crowded with wounded and the dying, they resembled floating hospitals, sending forth groans at every roll."

The brave Broke had received a severe wound in the head, and was lying delirious on board of his own vessel. He constantly inquired for the fate of his gallant adversary, and kept speaking of the "masterly style" in which the latter had brought the *Chesapeake* into action.

Lawrence, though conscious, sealed his lips and never spoke, though suffering great bodily pain, making no comment upon the battle. He lingered four days, and finally expired.

His body was wrapped in the colors of his ship and laid upon the quarter-deck of the *Chesapeake*, to be conveyed for burial to Halifax. At the time of his death he was but thirty-two years of age, sixteen years of which had been passed in the service of his country.

Great were the rejoicings at the British port when the two vessels sailed in, and our hearts cannot fail to be touched by the honors paid on this occasion by the British to the departed American hero.

His pall was borne by the oldest captains in the British service that were then in Halifax, and the naval officers crowded to yield the last honors to a man who had been so lately their foe. There is a sympathy between lofty souls that knows no distinction of clime or nation.

As usual, much controversy over the numbers engaged and the weight of armament was aroused.

So far as can be learned, the crews were nearly matched, each numbering about four hundred.

The *Shannon* lost twenty-four killed, including three officers, and fifty wounded. The *Chesapeake*, forty-seven killed and ninety-nine wounded.

Lawrence's first lieutenant was killed, and all the surviving lieutenants wounded, as were also five midshipmen and the chaplain.

Lieutenant William Cox, whose court-martial attracted much attention after the investigation into the loss of the *Chesapeake*, was doubtless a victim of the chagrin that the country felt at England's victory. Cox had fought bravely throughout the early part of the action, and there is much to prove that his going below with the wounded Lawrence was in compliance with the latter's orders.

Lieutenant Provo Wallis, who brought the *Chesapeake* as a prize into Halifax, died within the last few years, an admiral, the oldest naval officer then living in the service of Great Britain.

# IX
## THE "ENTERPRISE" AND THE "BOXER"
[September 5th, 1813]

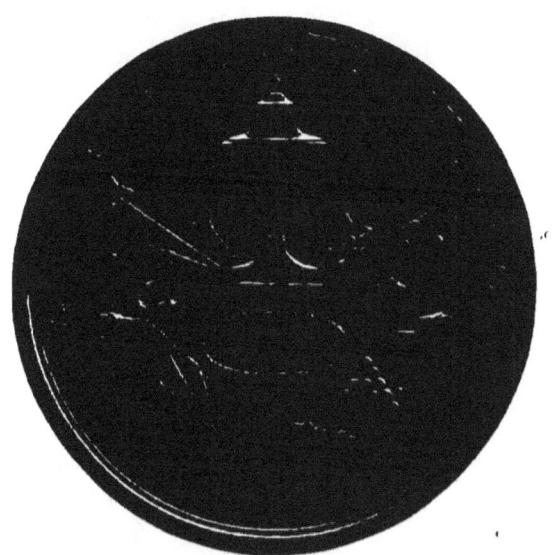

MEMORIAL MEDAL IN HONOR OF
CAPTAIN WILLIAM BURROWS

MEDAL PRESENTED BY CONGRESS TO
LIEUTENANT EDWARD R. M'CALL

WILLIAM BURROWS was one of those men from whose early training and development of character great things might have been expected. He was born in 1785, near Philadelphia, and as a boy he had marked peculiarities that presaged somewhat the eccentricities that were shown by him in after-life.

His father was wealthy, and, being a man of accomplished mind and polished manners, he determined to fit his son for no profession, but intended to give him the best education that could be had. But the boy seemed to show little desire to master that which would only fit him to enjoy the better a life of leisure. A desire for travel, a wild longing for the sea and for ships, manifested itself before he was twelve years old. He cherished a solitary independence of mind, and did not indulge in much of the playfulness or the pranks of boyhood.

At last, seeing that it was impossible to break him of his desire for a seafaring life, the whole course of his education was changed, and before he had trod the deck of a vessel he was instructed in naval science. This he took up with avidity, and the intense hatred for mathematics he had shown hitherto entirely disappeared. In November, 1799, a midshipman's warrant was procured for him, and the following January he joined the corvette *Portsmouth*, and sailed for France. He served on board various ships of war until 1803, when he was ordered to the frigate *Constitution*, under Commodore Preble. He distinguished himself in the Tripolitan war, and centred all his pride in becoming a thorough and accomplished sailor. Being mortified by the appointment of some junior officers over his head, he attempted to resign the service just previous to the outbreak of the second war with Great Britain; his resignation was not accepted. However, after much trouble, he received a furlough, and made a trip to China as first officer on board the merchant ship *Thomas Penrose*, which vessel he saved on one occasion by his good seamanship. What was his delight, upon coming back to his country, to find that his friends had been working for him, and that he had been appointed to the command of the brig *Enterprise*, 16 guns, at Portsmouth! His character immediately underwent a change. He threw off the misanthropic manner and the morose feelings that had characterized him, and showed such knowledge and despatch in outfitting his little brig that she was probably as well equipped as any vessel of her tonnage in any service, and her crew as well trained.

On the 1st of September the *Enterprise* sailed from Portsmouth on a cruise to the southward. She encountered light weather and baffling winds, and saw no sail until early on the morning of the 5th, when a brig was espied inshore getting under way. For some time the *Enterprise* tacked to and fro, unable to ascertain the character of the stranger. But soon all doubts were put aside by seeing the brig display two flags, one at each mast-head; and although some miles distant, she fired a gun, as if in challenge.

The *Enterprise* hauled up on the wind and stood out to sea, preparing for action. Then followed one of the strange circumstances which happened so often in those days. The wind died away, and for six hours or more the two enemies drifted about in a dead calm, watching each other through their glasses, and preparing for the conflict that would take place as soon as the breeze would enable them to lessen the distance between them.

At half-past two in the afternoon it came, from the southwest, a light wind that gave the *Enterprise* the advantage of the weather-gage. It took only a few minutes to find out that, so far as sailing went, the two vessels were on equal terms, and at 3 P.M. Burrows shortened sail, squared his yards, and bore down before the wind. He hoisted an ensign at each of his mast-heads and another at the peak, firing a gun to answer the previous challenge of the morning. Then, in silence, the two vessels neared. Closer and closer they came without a shot being fired, the men at the guns being eager to commence, and the officers anxiously awaiting word from the young commander (Burrows was but twenty-eight), who was walking quickly to and fro alone on the quarter-deck.

When within half pistol-shot the Englishman came up into the wind and gave three cheers, immediately letting go his starboard broadside. The cheers and the broadside were returned, and the action at once became general.

Burrows had the opportunity for which he had been praying. He noticed that the training of his crew was showing to good effect; all the care and trouble he had taken were now being paid for.

He had turned to speak to Lieutenant McCall, to attract attention to the way in which the enemy was being hulled, when a musket-ball struck him in the body, and he fell. McCall bent over him. "Don't take me below," he said, as he lay on the deck. "Never strike that flag."

Maybe the recollection of the words of the great Lawrence influenced him as he spoke. They brought a hammock from the nettings and placed it underneath his head, and McCall assumed the active command.

This had happened during the first eight minutes of the engagement, and so accurate was the gunnery of the Americans that the main-topmast and the topsail yard of the Englishman were soon shot away, and a position gained whence a raking fire was kept up for some twelve minutes.

Suddenly it was noticed that the enemy was not

THE "ENTERPRISE" HAILING THE "BOXER"

replying, although the colors were still flying at the mast-heads.

McCall gave orders to cease firing, and then through the smoke came a hoarse voice hailing the American brig. "Cease firing there!" it said. "We have surrendered."

"Why don't you haul down your colors?" returned McCall through the trumpet.

"We can't, sir. They are nailed to the mast," was the reply.

A boat was lowered from the *Enterprise*, and McCall climbed to the deck of his late antagonist. She proved to be His Britannic Majesty's brig *Boxer*, 14 guns, that a few minutes before had been commanded by Samuel Blyth, a brave officer, who burned to distinguish himself, and had gone into action determined to follow the example of Sir Philip Vere Broke, and lead "a captured Yankee into Halifax Harbor"—so he had expressed himself. But he had not lived to see the outcome of the action. At the same time that Burrows fell on board the *Enterprise*, Blyth was killed by a cannon-shot on the quarter-deck of the *Boxer*.

His first officer came back with Lieutenant McCall, and approached the wounded Burrows, who yet refused to be carried below. The doctor had pronounced that he had but a few hours at most to live.

When he received the sword of his enemy, he grasped it in both hands. "I am satisfied," he said;

and soon afterwards he was covered with the flag below in his own cabin—"a smile on his lips," wrote one of the officers.

As usual, much controversy was excited in regard to the numbers of crew and armament of the two vessels.

An extract from a letter from Commodore Hull to Commodore Bainbridge, dated September 10th, 1813, is of great interest. Hull writes:

> "I yesterday visited the two brigs, and was astonished to see the difference of injury sustained in the action. The *Enterprise* has but one eighteen-pound shot in her hull, one in her mainmast, and one in her foremast; her sails are much cut with grape-shot, but no injury was done by them.
>
> "The *Boxer* has eighteen or twenty eighteen-pound shot in her hull, most of them at the water's edge; several stands of grape-shot in her side, and such a quantity of smaller grape that I didn't undertake to count them. Her masts, sails, and spars are literally cut to pieces; several of her guns dismounted and unfit for service. To give an idea, I inform you that I counted in her mainmast alone three eighteen-pound shot-holes.
>
> "I find it impossible to get at the number killed, as no papers are found by which we can ascertain it. I, however, counted upwards of ninety hammocks that were in her nettings, besides several beds without hammocks. I have no doubt that she carried one hundred men on board."

The exact number on board the *Enterprise* was one hundred and two.

In addition to the particulars thus officially given, from other sources it was ascertained that the *Enterprise* rated as 12 guns, but carried 16—viz., 14 eighteen-pound carronades and 2 long nines;

her officers and crew consisted of one hundred and two persons, and her burden was about two hundred and sixty-five tons.

The *Boxer* rated as a 14-gun brig, but carried 18, disposed as follows: 16 eighteen-pound carronades in her broadsides and 2 long nines on deck. She was very heavily built, and was about three hundred tons in burden.

Soon after the arrival of the *Enterprise* and her prize at Portland the bodies of the two dead commanders were brought on shore in ten-oared barges rowed at minute strokes by masters of ships, and accompanied by a procession of almost all the barges and boats in the harbor. Minute-guns were fired from the vessels, the same ceremony was performed over each body, and the procession moved through the streets, preceded by the selectmen and the municipal officers, and guarded by the crew of the *Enterprise*, all the officers of that vessel and of the *Boxer* acting as joint mourners.

It is a strange fact that Burrows had never been in a battle before, and that McCall, on whom had devolved the responsibility of command, had never previously heard the sound of a hostile shot.

The losses during the action were, as near as could be ascertained, as follows:

The *Boxer*, twenty-eight killed and fourteen wounded; and the *Enterprise*, one killed and thirteen wounded, three of whom afterwards died.

# X
## THE BATTLE OF LAKE ERIE
[September 10th, 1813]

MEDAL PRESENTED BY CONGRESS TO
CAPTAIN OLIVER HAZARD PERRY

OLIVER HAZARD PERRY, the hero of Lake Erie, inherited from his father a fearless, high-strung disposition, and early in life showed his longing for adventure. The elder Perry was a seaman from the time he could lift a handspike, and fought in the revolutionary days, first as a privateersman on a Boston letter-of-marque, and afterwards as a volunteer on board the frigate *Trumbull* and the sloop of war *Mifflin*. He was captured and imprisoned for eight long months in the famous Jersey prison-ship, where he succeeded in braving the dangers of disease, starvation, and hardship, and at last regained his liberty. Once more he became a privateersman, but ill-fortune followed him. He was captured in the English Channel, and confined for eighteen months in a British prison, whence he again escaped and made his way to the island of St. Thomas. From thence he sailed to Charleston, South Carolina, where he arrived about the time that peace was concluded. After that Perry found employment in the East Indian trade until 1798, when he was appointed to the command of the U.S.S. *General Greene*. He was the head of a large family, having married in 1783, the oldest of his children being Oliver Hazard. Of the four other sons, three of them also entered the navy and served with distinction.

Oliver Hazard as a boy was not physically strong; he grew tall at an early age, and his strength was not in keeping with his inches. Nevertheless, he declared himself positively in favor of taking up the sea as a profession, and in April of 1799, after his father had been in command of the *General Greene* for one year, to his delight young Perry received his midshipman's warrant, and joined the same ship.

The young midshipman made several cruises with his father to the West Indies; his health and strength increased with the life in the open air; he showed capacity and courage, and participated in the action that resulted in the reduction of Jacmel in connection with the land attack of the celebrated General Toussaint's army. This was the last active service of the *General Greene;* she was sold and broken up, and upon the reduction of the navy in 1801 the elder Perry left the service. In 1803 his son returned from a cruise in the Mediterranean, and was promoted to an acting lieutenancy.

In our naval history of this time the recurrence of various names, and the references made over and over again to the same actions and occurrences, are easily accountable when we think of the small number of vessels the United States possessed and the surprisingly few officers on the pay-rolls. The high feeling of *esprit de corps* that existed among them came from the fact that they each had a chance to prove their courage and fidelity. There was a high standard set for them to reach.

Oliver Hazard Perry went through the same school that, luckily for us, graduated so many fine officers and sailors — that of the Tripolitan war. After he returned to America, at the conclusion of peace with Tripoli, he served in various capacities along the coast, proving himself an efficient leader upon more than one occasion. The first service upon which the young officer was employed after the commencement of the war with England was taking charge of a flotilla of gunboats stationed at Newport.

As this service was neither arduous nor calculated to bring chances for active employment in the way of fighting, time hung on his hands, and Perry chafed greatly under his enforced retirement. At last he petitioned the government to place him in active service, stating plainly his desire to be attached to the naval forces that were then gathering under the command of Commodore Chauncey on the lakes. His request was granted, to his great joy, and he set out with all despatch.

It was at an early period of the war that the government had seen the immense importance of gaining the command of the western lakes, and in October of 1812 Commodore Chauncey had been ordered to take seven hundred seamen and one hundred and fifty marines and proceed by forced marches to Lake

Ontario. There had been sent ahead of him a large number of ship-builders and carpenters, and great activity was displayed in building and outfitting a fleet which might give to the United States the possession of Lake Ontario. There was no great opposition made to the American arms by the British on this lake, but the unfortunate surrender of General Hull had placed the English in undisputed possession of Lake Erie.

In March, 1813, Captain Perry having been despatched to the port of Erie, arrived there to find a fleet of ten sail being prepared to take the waters against the British fleet under Commodore Barclay—an old and experienced leader, a hero of the days of Nelson and the *Victory*.

Before Perry's arrival a brilliant little action had taken place in October of the previous year. Two British vessels, the *Detroit* and the *Caledonia*, came down the lake and anchored under the guns of the British Fort Erie on the Canadian side. At that time Lieutenant Elliot was superintending the naval affairs on Lake Erie, and the news having been brought to him of the arrival of the English vessels on the opposite side, he immediately determined to make a night attack and cut them out. For a long time a body of seamen had been tramping their toilsome march from the Hudson River to the lakes, and Elliot, hearing that they were but some thirty miles away, despatched a messenger to hasten them forward; at the same time he began to prepare two small boats for the expedition. About twelve o'clock the wearied seamen, footsore and hungry, arrived, and then it was discovered that in the whole draft there were but twenty pistols, and no cutlasses, pikes, or battle-axes. But Elliot was not dismayed. Applying to General Smyth, who was in command of the regulars, for arms and assistance, he was supplied with a few muskets and pistols, and about fifty soldiers were detached to aid him.

Late in the afternoon Elliot had picked out his crews and manned the two boats, putting about fifty men in each; but he did not stir until one o'clock on the following morning, when in the pitch darkness he set out from the mouth of Buffalo Creek, with a long pull ahead. The wind was not strong enough to make good use of the sails, and the poor sailors were so weary that those who were not rowing lay sleeping, huddled together on their arms, and displaying great listlessness and little desire for fighting. At three o'clock Elliot was alongside the British vessels. It was a complete surprise; in ten minutes he had full possession of them and had secured the crews as prisoners. But after making every exertion to get under sail, he found to his bitter disappointment that the wind was unfortunately so light that the rapid current made them gather an increasing sternway every instant. Another unfortunate circumstance was that he would have to pass the British fort below and quite close to hand, for he was on the Canadian shore. As the vessels came in sight of the British battery, the latter opened a heavy fire of round and grape, and several pieces of flying artillery stationed in the woods took up the chorus.

The *Caledonia*, being a smaller vessel, succeeded in getting out of the current, and was beached in as safe a position as possible under one of the American batteries at Black Rock, across the river; but Elliot was compelled to drop his anchor at the distance of about four hundred yards from two of the British batteries. He was almost at their mercy, and in the extremity he tried the effect of a ruse, or, better, made a threat that we must believe he never intended carrying into effect.

Observing an officer standing on the top of an earthwork, he hailed him at the top of his voice:

"Heigh, there, Mr. John Bull! if you fire another gun at me I'll bring up all my prisoners, and you can use them for targets," he shouted.

The answer was the simultaneous discharge of all of the Englishman's guns. But not a single prisoner was brought on deck to share the fate of the Americans, who felt the effect of the fire, and who now began to make strenuous efforts to return it. Elliot brought all of the guns on one side of his ship, and replied briskly, until he suddenly discovered that all of his ammunition was expended. Now there was but one chance left: to cut the cable, drift down the river out of the reach of the heavy batteries, and make a stand against the flying artillery with small arms. This was accordingly done, but as the sails were raised the fact was ascertained that the pilot had taken French leave. No one else knew the channel, and, swinging about, the vessel drifted astern for some ten minutes, then, fortunately striking a cross current, she brought up on the shore of Squaw Island, near the American side. Elliot sent a boat to the mainland with the prisoners first. It experienced great difficulty in making the passage, being almost swamped once or twice, and it did not return. Affairs had reached a crisis, but with the aid of a smaller boat, and by the exercise of great care, the remainder of the prisoners and the crew succeeded in getting on shore at about eight o'clock in the morning. At about eleven o'clock a company of British regulars rowed over from the Canadian shore to Squaw Island and boarded the *Detroit*, their intention being to destroy her, and burn up the munitions with which she was laden. Seeing their purpose, Major Cyrenus Chapin, a good Yankee from Massachusetts, called for volunteers to return to the island, and, despite the difficulties ahead, almost every man signified his willingness to go. Quickly making his selection, Major Chapin succeeded in landing with about thirty men at his back, and drove off the English before they had managed to start the flames. About three o'clock a second attempt was made, but it was easily repulsed.

The *Detroit* mounted six long 6-pounders, and her crew numbered some sixty men. She was worth saving, but so badly was she grounded on the island that it was impossible to get her off, and, after taking her stores out, Elliot set her on fire to get rid of her. The little *Caledonia* was quite a valuable capture, aside from her armament, as she had on board a cargo of furs whose value has been estimated at one hundred and fifty thousand dollars.

But to return to the condition of affairs upon the arrival of Captain Perry. The fleet that in a few weeks he had under his command consisted of the brig *Lawrence*, of 20 guns, to which he attached his flag; the *Niagara*, of 20 guns, in command of Elliot; and the schooners *Caledonia* and *Ariel*, of 3 and 4 guns respectively. There were besides six smaller vessels, carrying from one to two guns each; in all, Perry's fleet mounted 55 guns. The British fleet, under command of Barclay, consisted of the *Detroit* (named after the one that was wrecked), the *Queen Charlotte*, and the *Lady Prevost*. They mounted 19, 17, and 13 guns, in the order named. The brig *Hunter* carried 10 guns; the sloop *Little Belt*, 3; and the schooner *Chippeway*, 1 gun; in all, Barclay had 63 guns, not counting several swivels— that is, more than eight guns to the good.

The morning of the 10th of September dawned fine and clear. Perry, with his fleet anchored about him, lay in the quiet waters of Put-in Bay. A light breeze was blowing from the south. Very early a number of sail were seen out on the lake beyond the point, and soon the strangers were discovered to be the British fleet. Everything depended now upon the speed, with which the Americans could prepare for action. In twelve minutes every vessel was under way and sailing out to meet the oncomers; the *Lawrence* led the line. As the two fleets approached, the British concentrated the fire of their long and heavy guns upon her. She came on in silence; at her peak was flying a huge mottoflag; plain to view were the words of the brave commander of the *Chesapeake:* "Don't give up the ship."

The responsibility that rested upon the young commander's shoulders was great; his position was most precarious. This was the first action between the fleets of the two hostile countries; it was a battle for the dominion of the lakes; defeat meant that the English could land at any time an expeditionary force at any point they chose along the shores of our natural northern barrier. . The *Lawrence* had slipped quite a way ahead of the others, and Perry found that he would have to close, in order to return the English fire, as at the long distance he was surely being ripped to pieces.

Signalling the rest of the fleet to follow him, he made all sail and bore down upon the English; but to quote from the account in the *Naval Temple*, printed in the year 1816: "Every brace and bowline of the *Lawrence* being shot away, she became unmanageable, notwithstanding the great exertion of the sailing-master. In this situation she sustained the action within canister distance upwards of two hours, until every gun was rendered useless, and the greater part of her crew either killed or wounded."

It is easy to imagine the feelings of Perry at this moment. The smaller vessels of his fleet had not come within firing distance; there was absolutely nothing for him to do on board the flagship except to lower his flag. Yet there was one forlorn hope that occurred to the young commander, and without hesitation he called away the only boat capable of floating; taking his flag, he quitted the *Lawrence*, and rowed off for the *Niagara*. The most wonderful accounts of hair-breadth escapes could not equal that of Perry upon this occasion. Why his boat was not swamped, or its crew and commander killed, cannot be explained. Three of the British ships fired broadsides at him at pistol-shot distance, as he passed by them in succession; and although the water boiled about him, and the balls whistled but a few inches overhead, he reached the *Niagara* in safety.

There are but a few parallel cases to this, of a commander leaving one ship and transferring his flag to another in the heat of action.

The Duke of York upon one occasion shifted his flag, in the battle of Solebay; and in the battle of Texel, fought on August 11, 1673, the English Admiral Sprague shifted his flag from the *Royal*

THE "NIAGARA" BREAKS THE ENGLISH LINE

*Prince* to the *St. George*, and the Dutch Admiral Van Tromp shifted his flag from the *Golden Lion* to the *Comet*, owing to the former vessel being practically destroyed by a concentrated fire. This does not detract from the gallantry of Perry's achievement. The danger he faced was great, and he was probably closer to the enemy's vessels than any of the commanders above mentioned.

Perry's younger brother, who was but a midshipman, was one of the seven other men in the boat. They left on board the *Lawrence* not above a halfscore of able-bodied men to look after the numerous wounded. Owing to the opinions of many of the contemporary writers, who gave way to an intense feeling of partisanship, some bitterness was occasioned, and sides were taken in regard to the actions of Master Commandant Elliot and his superior officer; but looking back at it from this day, we can see little reason for any feeling of jealousy. It is hard to point the finger at any one on the American side in this action and say that he did not do his duty. As Perry reached the side of the *Niagara* the wind died away until it was almost calm; the smaller vessels, the sloops and schooners—the *Somers*, the *Scorpion*, the *Tigress*, the *Ohio*, and the *Porcupine*—were seen to be well astern. Upon Perry setting foot on deck, Elliot congratulated him upon the way he had left his ship, and volunteered to bring up the boats to windward, if he could be spared. Upon receiving permission he jumped into the boat in which Perry had rowed from the *Lawrence*, and set out to bring up all the forces. Every effort was made to form a front of battle, and the little gunboats, urged on by sweeps and oars, were soon engaged in a race for glory. In the meantime, however, the English had slackened their fire as they saw the big flag lowered from the *Lawrence's* masthead; they supposed that the latter had struck, and set up a tremendous cheering. This was hushed as they caught sight of the flash of oars and realized what was going forward. In a few minutes out of the thick smoke came the *Niagara*, breaking their line, and firing her broadsides with such good execution that great confusion followed throughout the fleet. Two of their larger brigs, the *Queen Charlotte* and *Detroit*, ran afoul of each other, and the *Niagara*, giving signal for close action, ran across the bow of one ship and the stern of the other, raking them both with fearful effect; then squaring away, and running astern of the *Lady Prevost*, she got in another raking fire, and, sheering off, made for the *Hunter*. Now the little 1-gun and 2-gun vessels of the American fleet were giving good accounts of themselves.

Although their crews were exposed to full view and stood waist-high above the bulwarks, they did no dodging; their shots were well directed, and they raked the Englishmen fore and aft, carrying away all the masts of the *Detroit* and the mizzenmast of the *Queen Charlotte*.

A few minutes after 3 P.M., a white flag at end of a boarding-pike was lifted above the bulwarks of the *Hunter*. At the sight of this the *Chippeway* and *Little Belt* crowded all sail and tried to escape, but in less than a quarter of an hour they were captured and brought back by the *Trippe* and the *Scorpion*, under the commands of Lieutenant Thomas Holdup and Sailing-master Stephen Champlin. With a ringing cheer the word went through the line that the British had surrendered. The sovereignty of Lake Erie belonged to America. The question of supremacy was settled.

The events of the day had been most dramatic. This fight amid the wooded shores and extending arms of the bay was viewed from shore by hundreds of anxious Americans. The bright sunlight and calm surface of the lake, the enshrouding fog of smoke that from shore hid all but the spurts of flame and the topmasts and occasionally the flags of the vessels engaged, all had combined to make a drama of the most exciting and awe-inspiring interest. Nor was the last act to be a letting down. Perry determined to receive the surrender of the defeated enemy nowhere else but on the deck of his old flag-ship that was slowly drifting up into the now intermingled fleets.

Once more he lowered his broad pennant, and rowed out for the crippled *Lawrence*. He was received on board with three feeble cheers, the wounded joining in, and a number of men crawling up from the slaughter-pen of a cockpit, begrimed and bloody.

On board the *Lawrence* there had been left but one surgeon, Usher Parsons. He came on deck red to the elbows from his work below, and the terrible execution done by the concentrated English fire was evident to the English officers as they stepped on board the flag-ship. Dead men lay everywhere. A whole gun's crew were littered about alongside of their wrecked piece. From below came the mournful howling of a dog. The cockpit had been above the water's surface, owing to the *Lawrence's* shallow draught, and here was a frightful sight. The wounded had been killed outright or wounded again as they lay on the surgeon's table. Twice had Perry called away the surgeon's aids to help work ship, and once his hail of "Can any wounded men below there pull a rope?" was answered by three or four brave, mangled fellows crawling up on deck to try to do their duty. All this was apparent to the English officers as they stepped over the bodies of the dead and went aft to where Perry stood with his arms folded, no vainglorious expression on his face, but one of sadness for the deeds that had been done that day. Each of the English officers in turn presented his sword, and in reply Perry bowed and requested that the side-arms should be retained. As soon as the formalities had been gone through with, Perry tore off the back of an old letter he took from his pocket, and, using his stiff hat for a writing-desk, scribbled the historic message which a detractor has charged he cribbed from Julius Cæsar: "We have met the enemy and they are ours:—two ships, two brigs, one schooner, and one sloop."

Calling away a small boat, he sent Midshipman Forrest with the report to General William Henry Harrison.

A computation has been made by one historian of the number of guns directed against the *Lawrence* in the early part of the action. The English had heavier armaments and more long guns; they could fight at a distance where the chubby carronade was useless. The *Lawrence* had but seven guns whose shots could reach her opponents, while the British poured into her the concentrated fire of thirty-two! This accounts for the frightful carnage.

When the *Lawrence* was being shot through and through, and there were but three guns that could reply to the enemy's fire, Lieutenant Yarnell, disfigured by a bad wound across his face from a splinter, came up to where Perry was standing. "The officers of my division have all been cut down," he said. "Can I have others?" Perry looked about him and sent three of his aids to help Yarnell, but in less than a quarter of an hour the lieutenant returned again. His words were almost the same as before, but he had a fresh wound in his shoulder. "These officers," he said, "have been cut down also."

"There are no more," Perry replied. "Do your best without them."

Three times was Yarnell wounded, and three times after his wounds had been hurriedly dressed he returned to his post.

Dulany Forrest, the midshipman whom Perry sent with the despatch to General Harrison, had a most remarkable escape. He was a brave lad who had faced death before; he had seen the splinters fly in the action between the *Constitution* and the *Java*. Forrest was standing close to Captain Perry when a grape-shot that had glanced from the side of a port struck the mast, and, again deflected, caught the midshipman in the chest. He fell, gasping, at Perry's feet.

"Are you badly hurt, lad?" asked the latter, anxiously, as he raised the midshipman on his knee.

"No, sir; not much," the latter answered, as he caught his breath. "But this is my shot, I think." And with that he extracted the half-spent ball from his clothing and slipped it into his pocket.

Midshipman Henry Laub was killed in the cockpit just after having had a dressing applied to his shattered right arm. A Narragansett Indian who served as a gunner in the forward division of the *Lawrence* was killed in the same manner.

A summary of the losses on both sides shows that, despite the death-list of the *Lawrence*, the English loss was more severe. On board the American flag-ship twenty-two were killed and sixty-one were wounded. On board the *Niagara* two killed and twenty-five wounded. The *Ariel* had one killed and three wounded. The *Scorpion*, two killed. The *Caledonia*, three wounded; and the *Somers* and *Trippe* each showed but two wounded men apiece. In all, twenty-seven were killed and ninety-six wounded on the American side. The comparison of the loss of the rest of the fleet and that suffered by the *Lawrence* makes a remarkable showing. The English lost forty-one killed and ninety-four wounded altogether. A number of Canadian Indians were found on board the English vessels. They had been engaged as marksmen, but the first shot had taken all the fight out of them and they had hidden and skulked for safety.

Perry's treatment of the prisoners was magnanimous. Everything that would tend to relieve the sufferings of the wounded was done, and relief was distributed impartially among the sufferers on both sides. The result of this action was a restoration of practical peace along the frontier of the lake. The British evacuated Detroit and Michigan, and the dreaded invasion of the Indians that the settlers had feared so long was headed off.

Perry, who held but a commission of master commandant, despite his high acting rank, was promoted at once to a captaincy, the date of his commission bearing the date of his victory. He was given the command of the frigate *Java*, a new 44-gun ship then fitting out at Baltimore. Gold medals were awarded to him and to Elliot by Congress, and silver medals to each of the commissioned officers. A silver medal also was given to the nearest male relative of Lieutenant Brooks of the marines, and swords to the nearest male relatives of Midshipmen Laub, Claxton, and Clark. Three months' extra pay was voted to all the officers, seamen, and marines, and, in addition, Congress gave $225,000 in prize-money, to be divided among the American forces engaged in the action. This sum was distributed in the following proportions: Commodore Chauncey, who was in command on the lakes, $12,750; Perry and Elliot, $7140 each—besides which Congress voted Perry an additional $5000; the commanders of gunboats, lieutenants, sailing-masters, and lieutenants of marines received $2295 each; midshipmen, $811; petty officers, $447 per capita; and marines and sailors, $209 apiece.

No money, however, could repay the brave men for the service they had rendered the country. To-day the dwellers along the shores of Lake Erie preserve the anniversary of the battle as an occasion for rejoicing. While the naval actions at sea reflected honor and glory to their commanders and credit to the service, the winning of the battle of Lake Erie averted a national catastrophe.

# XI
# THE DEFENCE
# OF THE "GENERAL ARMSTRONG"
[September 26th, 1814]

SAMUEL CHESTER REID was born at Norwich, Connecticut, in August, 1783. Like the majority of the commanders who gained renown during the war of 1812, his sea-faring life began at a very early age. At eleven years he made his first voyage, and shortly afterwards he was captured by a French privateer, and for some time confined in the prison at Basseterre. He was released after six months' imprisonment, and, turning towards the regular navy, he served as acting midshipman on the U.S.S. *Baltimore*, and saw a good bit of active service with the squadron under Commodore Truxton in the West Indies.

As he held no regular commission in the service, he saw the great chance and opportunity presented for privateering enterprise, and took command of the *General Armstrong*, privateer. Her cruises were uniformly successful, and had it not been that circumstances forced her into national prominence she would probably have been forgotten like a hundred others of her class that had a vogue at the time. They enjoyed the popularity of the successful actor, but their names have gone out of people's memories after their short careers of glory.

But there has probably been as much writing

done about the wonderful defence of the *General Armstrong*, under Captain Samuel Reid, as there has been about any action in which ships of our regular navy participated. Captain Reid died in 1861, but even after his death the "*Armstrong* affair" was long kept before the public mind, owing to the claims of the heirs of the owners of the American vessel for damages against the Portuguese government.

The *General Armstrong* was a fast-sailing, cleverly handled little vessel, and she sailed from the port of New York, her crew having been recruited there. It was a motley gathering, as a great many of the crews of these vessels were, being composed of the pick of the merchant service, a few down-east fishermen, and, not strange to relate, adventurers of every sort and description, who, however, proved themselves to be great fighters when under competent leadership. Her full complement was about ninety men. The brig's armament was rather a peculiar one; she carried no carronades, but had three long nines on either side, and a long 24-pounder amidships. She could fight at a greater distance than many of the vessels belonging to the regular service.

Farragut in his journal mentions that when he was a midshipman of the *Essex*, sailing from New York, a sail was sighted off the weather beam. To the surprise of the officers she was carrying more canvas than might have been considered prudent considering the weather, but she stood up under it and legged it so fast that she soon came within hailing distance of the *Essex*. The latter vessel, not knowing her character, had her men at quarters. All the officers admired the way the little brig was handled. Upon speaking her she proved to be the *General Armstrong*, bound upon her second cruise into British waters—her first had been most successful.

But to the event which has handed her name down to history. On September 26th, 1814, the *General Armstrong* came to anchor in the Portuguese harbor of Fayal. At about sunset of the same day three large ships, flying the British flag, were seen to enter the roads.

As the privateer lay some distance out and it was dead calm within the harbor, Captain Reid deemed it wise to trust entirely to the neutrality of the port, and to claim the protection that should be given to any vessel by a neutral power.

As darkness fell he saw some suspicious actions on the part of the British ships—the *Carnation* coming as close as pistol-shot range, and the others approaching to a distance of less than two miles; through the glass Reid could see that boats were being lowered. He trusted, however, for some time in the good faith and justice of the British captains, but these preparations suggested no peaceful intentions, and he began to warp his brig closer in to shore, anchoring at last, stem and stern, under the very guns of the castle that commanded the harbor.

Calling his men on deck, he told them that he thought that the British intended, if possible, to cut him out. At once the temper of the crew was evident. A boatswain's mate approached him, and, saluting, said: "You can trust in us, sir. What you *say* we *do*."

It was growing dusk. At about eight o'clock Captain Reid plainly saw four boats filled with armed men row down towards him. As soon as they were within hailing distance he stepped upon the bulwarks, and, making a trumpet of his hands, he shouted: "Boats there! Approach no nearer; for your safety I warn you."

The rowing ceased, and there was evidently a consultation among the officers in command. Captain Reid's men were standing at their quarters. Two of the guns were heavily loaded with grape. After talking a few minutes it was evident that the English decided to risk the venture, for the oars caught the water at once, and they came dashing on towards the American vessel. All dissembling was laid aside, and Reid ordered his men to fire. Two of the boats mounted swivels forward and returned shots in answer. A discharge of small-arms also began, but the torrent of grape that had raked one of the cutters had killed a first lieutenant and several of his men, and most of the others were wounded. The boats swung back, and made for the sanctuary of the vessels in the harbor.

The moon had now risen, and it was very light.

## THE DEFENCE OF THE "GENERAL ARMSTRONG" 163

Large crowds had gathered on the shore, but the castle displayed no intention of taking any part in the affair.

The commanders of His Britannic Majesty's ships *Plantagenet*, *Rota*, and *Carnation* held a consultation. It resulted in a "most outrageous violation of the neutrality of a friendly port, and utter contempt of the laws of civilized nations," to quote from the report of John G. Dabney, American consul at Fayal.

Angered at the result of their first attempt, the English threw all caution aside. They crowded as many men as possible into all the boats they had, armed them with carronades, swivels, and small-arms, and once more rowed down in two divisions; but Reid was waiting for them. The guns were double-shotted, and he moved two of the long nines from the other side across the deck and cut ports for them in the bulwarks. A tremendous action now began, which lasted about forty minutes. Never in any of the hostile meetings between the frigates or the fleets of the United States and England has such destruction and carnage been recorded, in proportion to the number engaged, as is shown by the loss of the British on this occasion. The fire from the brig cut away whole boats' crews and almost destroyed the boats. It is estimated that about 400 men were divided among the flotilla of the attacking party. They fought bravely, but there is merit in being well prepared for defence. More than half of the British were either killed or wounded, "Long Tom," the 25-pounder, doing terrible execution.

The outmost boats showed signs of giving up the contest. Those nearer the *General Armstrong* continued to fight desperately, but none had approached near enough to cut their way through the boarding nettings which Reid had strung along the sides.

Seeing that there was an intention to retire, if possible, on the part of the British, he slackened his fire. Two boats were drifting, however, beneath the quarter of the privateer. They were loaded with their own dead. From these two boats only seventeen men reached shore alive, and, with the exception of three, all of these were wounded.

The following day, from dawn until sunset, the British were occupied in burying their dead, among them being two lieutenants, one midshipman of the *Rota*, and the first lieutenant of the *Plantagenet*, who died of his wounds. The British endeavored to conceal the extent of the loss, but even they admit that they lost in killed and those who died of their wounds afterwards upward of one hundred and twenty-five officers and men.

The captain of the *Rota*, in his report, stated that he lost seventy men from his own ship.

It was claimed by the English that the first expedition of four boats, which was sent out early in the evening of the 26th, was merely a reconnoitring party, and had no hostile intentions; but it seemed a strange thing to reconnoitre at night an enemy's vessel in a friendly port with one hundred and twenty armed men, a third as many again as were on board the American brig. There is no question, viewing the proceedings dispassionately, that they had hoped to take Reid by surprise.

To quote from Dabney's report once more: "In vain can he [the British commander] expect by such subterfuge to shield himself from the indignation of the world and the merited resentment of his own government and nation for thus trampling on the sovereignty of their most ancient and faithful ally, and for the wanton sacrifice of British lives."

The comparison of the loss sustained by the American and by the British sides is almost ridiculous—on the *Armstrong* two were killed and seven wounded. One of the former was Alexander O. Williams, of New York, the second lieutenant, an officer of bravery and merit. The first and third lieutenants, Messrs. Worth and Johnson, were wounded, and thus, strange to say, Captain Reid was deprived of the services of all of his junior officers, and was forced to conduct the defence alone.

The next morning one of the British ships took advantage of the wind which sprang up, and, sailing in, commenced a heavy cannonade upon the privateer. Captain Reid replied for a few moments, but finding of course that the result of final capture was inevitable, owing to the fact that the other vessels displayed intentions of joining in, he decided to abandon the *General Armstrong*. He hove his guns and powder overboard, and, manning his boats, brought his crew ashore.

As soon as the *Armstrong* was abandoned the British took possession of her, but, finding that she had been partially destroyed, out of revenge immediately set fire to her.

Dabney, in his letter to the Secretary of State, remarks as follows: " At nine o'clock in the evening (soon after the first attack) I called on the Governor, requesting his Excellency to protect the privateer, either by force or by such remonstrance to the commander of the squadron as would cause him to desist from any further attempt. The Governor, indignant at what had passed, but feeling himself totally unable, with the slender means he possessed, to resist such a force, took the part of remonstrating, which he did in forcible but respectful terms. His letter to Captain Lloyd had no other effect than to produce a menacing reply, insulting in the highest degree. Nothing can exceed the indignation of the public authorities, as well as of all ranks and descriptions of persons here, at this unprovoked enormity. Such was the rage of the British to destroy this vessel that no regard was paid to the safety of the town. Some of the inhabitants were wounded, and a number of houses were much damaged. The strongest representations on this subject are prepared by the Governor for his court."

Now followed one of the strangest incidents that occurred during our last war with England. The senior commander, Captain Lloyd, threatened to send on shore an armed force to arrest the crew of the privateer, claiming that Englishmen were among them; but the *General Armstrong's* people fled to the mountains, and some of them took possession of an old church, preparing to defend themselves. Lloyd was fearful of losing more men if he tried to force this point; so, resorting to stratagem, he addressed an official letter to the Governor, stating that in the American crew were two men deserters from his own squadron, and who were thus guilty of high-treason. Under this claim a force was sent into the country by the Portuguese. The American seamen were arrested and brought to town, but the pretended deserters could not be found. All the seamen, however, had to pass under the humiliating examination of the British officers.

It was a fortunate thing that the erroneous statement of Captain Lloyd resulted in nothing more serious than this.

Reid protested against the actions of the commanders of the British squadron, and also against the government of Portugal for not protecting him, and it was on this protest that the wearisome waiting and lawsuits arose which became known as the "Armstrong claims," and which were decided unfortunately against the Americans by Louis Napoleon, who was chosen arbiter. The " Long Tom " was presented to America by the Portuguese three years ago, and was exhibited at the World's Fair in Chicago.

# XII
## THE LOSS OF THE "ESSEX"
[March 28th, 1814]

LATE in the fall of 1813 a little American brig made her way up the coast with a cargo that had once been consigned to some British merchants in the West Indies.

The little brig had also, a few months previously, flown the British flag, but now she came drifting into the harbor of New York under a prize-master and his crew, for she had been taken in the Gulf of Mexico by one of the privateers that had outfitted from New York.

She brought the news that only a short time before her capture three smart English vessels had stopped at the port in which she had lain at anchor. Two of these three vessels were sent from England on a special mission; it was intended that they should round the Horn and cruise in company in the Pacific Ocean in search of the frigate *Essex*, that had spread terror from China to South America, and had chased the British shipping off the western ocean.

On the 27th of October, 1812, the *Essex*, under the command of David Porter, a fearless and persistent fighter, had set sail from the United States on a cruise to the southward, his orders being to join Bainbridge, his superior in the *Constitution*.

The coast of Brazil was then the cruising-ground for a large force of English ships of war.

Porter, hearing that Bainbridge, after his action with the *Java*, had been forced to return to the United States, determined to make his way around the continent into the blue waters of the Pacific. He had made one important capture a few days before arriving at this last decision, having taken the *Nocton*, one of King George's packets. On board of her were found eleven thousand pounds in specie.

After suffering severe hardships and meeting with many adverse winds and tides in rounding the Horn, Porter at last made his way along the harborless western coast, and arrived at Valparaiso on the 14th of March, 1813.

The *Essex's* crew had been on short allowance of water and small rations, but not a murmur of dissatisfaction had been raised throughout the voyage.

Having rested and victualled his ship, in a short time Porter hoisted his anchors, spread his sails, and sailed out to sea again.

He had been out but a few days when he came across a Peruvian corsair. Ordering her to heave to, he boarded her, and found, to his astonishment, that she had on board twenty-four American sailors, the crews of two whaling ships which she had taken on the coast of Chili. When asked to explain his conduct, the Peruvian captain answered that, in view of the fact that his country was an ally of Great Britain, and that war was soon to be declared between

Spain and America, he had taken matters into his own hand. Porter, much incensed, released the American sailors, and having thrown all the ammunition and guns of the rather previous pirate overboard, he was let go, with a letter to the Viceroy, complaining of his conduct.

Just before the *Essex* entered the harbor of Lima she overhauled one of the corsair's prizes, replaced her crew on board of her, and sent them on their way to New Bedford rejoicing.

For a year the *Essex* cruised up and down the coast of South America, extending her voyages far to the westward, to the various islands, which were visited then infrequently by traders and whaling vessels.

During this cruise she frightened British commerce entirely from these waters, and the strange spectacle of seeing one ship in control of a vast territory was presented to the eyes of the world. The British Admiralty were vexed and astounded beyond measure. Here one day and there the next, Porter appeared to be in command of a fleet instead of a single frigate.

He had fitted one of the captured British whalers as a tender, and named her the *Essex Junior*, placing her under the command of Lieutenant Downes, giving her an armament of ten 18-pound carronades and ten short sixes, with a complement of sixty men.

At last, tiring of capturing merchantmen and glutted with the spoils of easy victories, Porter decided to look for larger game; for the news had been brought to him that the vessels which the little brig had reported at New York so long before were on their way, sailing under orders to find him at all hazards.

His ship required repairing, and therefore he sailed, accompanied by his convoy of prizes, to the island of Nookaheeva, one of the Washington group, that had been discovered by Captain Ingraham, of Boston. Porter took possession in the name of the United States, renaming it "Madison Island."

Here he cached many of his stores, and anchored three of the prizes well inshore. Erecting a small battery in a good position to command the small harbor, Lieutenant Gamble, of the marines, and twenty-one men were left with orders to proceed to Valparaiso after a certain period. Two of the captures were given up to the prisoners and sent to England. Three had been sent to America, and some were already anchored in the neutral port of Valparaiso. It was December 12th when Porter set sail from Madison Island for the coast of Chili. The *Essex Junior* followed in his wake.

He arrived safely in the harbor, and had been there but a short time, overhauling his spars and running-gear, when two sail came in from the westward; they were the *Phœbe*, under the command of Captain Hillyar, and the *Cherub*, sloop of war—both strongly armed and manned with picked crews—

the very ships that had been sent out to look for the *Essex*.

No sooner had they come into sight of the long headland than they found the frigate they were so eager to meet, within a short distance of them. Then it was plain that they were not going to allow her to escape.

The British vessels, as they came down the harbor upon their first entrance, sailed quite close to the American — so close, indeed, that, in endeavoring to come about, the *Phœbe* missed stays and fell afoul of the *Essex*, presenting herself in position to be raked fore and aft; but Porter respected the neutrality of the port and restrained his fire.

Had he known what was going to happen within the next few weeks, there probably would have been a different termination to the *Essex's* glorious cruise.

The divisions were all at quarters, matches burning, and it was with difficulty that the feverish seamen could be held in check.

So close were the ships that the men standing at the guns on the British vessels could be easily seen, even taunts were exchanged and grimaces were made over the bulwarks and through the open ports.

Sailing across to the other side of the harbor, and tacking again, the British vessels anchored near the entrance.

Now for some time ensued a remarkable condition of affairs. The commanders met on shore and exchanged gravely the courtesies which navy men extended to one another in those days, belligerents though they were. The shore parties of both forces meeting in town, under strict orders, for a wonder, managed to keep from fighting, but they were itching to be at it.

Porter had long flown a flag of his own with the motto, "Free Trade and Sailors' Rights."

But, as if not to be outdone, the British commander threw to the air his strips of bunting with a motto of his own: "God and Country. British Sailors' Best Rights. Traitors Offend Both." (It was a fallacy of the British that our ships were manned by deserters from the royal service.)

The sail-maker and his assistant were soon at work on board the American, and from the mizzen-mast of the *Essex* appeared the next morning:

"God, Our Country, and Liberty. Tyrants Offend Them."

Many times had Porter tried to get a challenge from Captain Hillyar (as the *Essex* was the weaker vessel, he was not in a position to offer the challenge himself), and he let it be well understood that he would meet the *Phœbe*, in open combat, and would agree that the *Essex Junior* should take no hand, on the condition that the *Cherub* also should remain inactive.

The prudence of Captain Hillyar cannot but be commended. He was under strict orders not to run any risks; he knew his enemy was at his mercy;

but the *Essex* had been put down, as most of our cruisers were in those days, as "a dangerous nondescript," to quote from the British press of the time. In fact, many British frigates in the Atlantic waters, where the *Constitution* had gained her laurels, kept near to the great towering battle-ships—guard-ships, they were called.

It was all arranged that if the *Essex* should show a tendency to make her way to sea, the *Phœbe* and *Cherub* would attack her simultaneously. That was their idea in sailing in each other's company.

Fearing that Porter might take advantage of a favorable wind to slip past them if they remained at anchor, Captain Hillyar left the harbor, and with the *Phœbe* proceeded to sea, where both ships patrolled up and down like sentries at a prison gate.

The united force of the English vessels amounted to eighty-one guns and five hundred men, in addition to which they had taken on board for the nonce the crew of an English letter-of-marque that was then lying in port.

The force of the *Essex* consisted of 46 guns, all of which, except six long twelves, were 32-pound carronades, and useless except in close fighting. Her crew, much reduced by the manning of her many prizes, consisted of but two hundred and fifty men. The armament of the *Essex Junior* we have named before.

It was evident that as long as the British vessels remained where they were, the *Essex* was as good as captured. Something must be done, and with such a commander as Porter the boldest plan was the most attractive.

Many incidents had occurred to break the monotony of the blockade. Many times had he left his anchorage, spread his sails, and made a feint of leaving the harbor, and in all these trials he had found that his ship could give the others points and beat them, so far as sailing went.

On one occasion the British ships stood boldly in before the wind and bore down upon the *Essex*, part of whose crew had been given shore leave; but before the tars had gone far into the town they saw the approaching sails, and some crowded into the little native boats that were hauled up along the shore; many even started to swim back to their vessel.

The drum rolled and flags went up to the *Essex's* mast-heads; but Hillyar at that moment respected the international law, hauled his wind, and went back to his blockading.

After a consultation with Lieutenant Downs, it was decided by Porter that the period of inaction must be broken. A rendezvous was appointed, and it was agreed that the *Essex* should allow the British ships to chase her offshore, and give the *Essex Junior* a chance to make her escape.

The very next day after arriving at this decision the wind came on to blow fresh from the southward, and then followed a chapter of accidents as disastrous as ever happened to any one unlucky vessel.

Even in yacht-racing the best boat does not always win; no allowances are made for accidents, hard luck is an element that cannot be forestalled, and thus it will always be in naval warfare. It must be confessed that the fates were against America on this day, the 28th of March.

The wind, which had started with a fresh breeze, grew stronger and stronger, and, the anchorage being hard ground, the *Essex* began to drag her anchors seaward. Suddenly her larboard cable parted, and she went, stern foremost, at a good rate of speed towards the harbor entrance. The adventure could be put off no longer. Trusting in the superior sailing of the *Essex* to be able to work to windward, Porter hoisted his topgallant-sails, braced around his yards, and came close upon the wind.

The British vessels, off to leeward, crowded on all sail. In the white-caps there was very little sea, for the fitful wind was new and off the land.

It looked as if the *Essex* were going to escape; but just as she rounded the point, the muzzles of her guns almost in the water, another link in the chain of unfortunate circumstances was forged; there was a crash, and the main-topmast went by the board, broken short above the top. The men who were then lying out upon the yards went down with the great spar over the side, and all were drowned. The *Essex* brought up as if she had struck a shoal.

The English ships were now coming fast. Porter had no alternative but to endeavor to get back to the protection of the port; but he could not reach his former anchorage, hampered as he was by the wreckage at his side. Therefore he made secure all sail upon his foremast and ran for shore, anchoring there about a pistol-shot distance from the beach, and three-quarters of a mile to leeward of the battery on the east side of the harbor. Here he worked industriously to clear his decks and cut away the tangled wreckage, but in the midst of this the crew of the *Essex* saw that they were not to be unmolested.

Hillyar had determined to take advantage of the moment the *Phœbe* and *Cherub* came down before the breeze, which was now dying away, and, breaking all precedent of neutrality, they opened up their broadsides upon their almost helpless antagonist. It was nearly four o'clock when the first gun was fired.

Porter, seeing that the action was going to begin, endeavored to get a spring upon his cable, and bring a broadside to bear upon the British ships. He hoisted every flag he had, at every point where he could reeve a halyard, awaiting quietly the nearer onslaught, and praying for close quarters.

The *Phœbe* placed herself under the stern, and the *Cherub* on his starboard bow; but so hot was the *Essex's* answer to the latter that she bore up and ran under his stern also; and now followed such slaughter as has hardly been equalled in naval warfare. From their positions they raked the hull of the *Essex* through and through, cutting long gashes in her sides, and aiming with precision, as if they were firing for practice at a helpless hull. Against all this destructive cannonade Porter could only bring to bear three long 12-pounders, which he had run out of the stern ports and the cabin-windows, and well were they manned and served.

Two or three times did he manage to get a spring upon his cable, and had half turned his broadside towards the enemy, but every time was the hawser shot away, and the poor ship drifted back to her almost defenceless position. Some of the round shot and whole charges of grape from the *Phœbe's* guns swept the *Essex's* decks from stern-post to the heel of her bowsprit. Whole crews were slaughtered as they worked the few guns able to be brought to bear; but as fast as the men were shot or blown away their places were filled by others. At one gun fifteen men were killed, and as many wounded and carried below.

At this point in the combat Hillyar signalled the *Cherub*, and they both drew off to repair their damages, that were far from slight.

Again in a few minutes they came down before the wind, and took a new position athwart the *Essex's* bows. To this fire Porter could not bring a single gun to answer. Again the decks of the *Essex* were red with blood; there had been no time to move the wounded, and the dead lay huddled about in all directions. Now the shots even entered the cockpit, and the men were killed as they lay on the operating-tables under the doctor's knife. To add to the horror, the *Essex* had caught on fire forward and aft.

Still undismayed, Porter determined to close with the enemy. The only sail that could be hoisted, owing to the mangled condition of the rigging, was the flying-jib. He raised this, cut his cable, and ran down on both ships, with the intention of boarding the *Phœbe* if possible.

At the prospect of being able to fight back, his men revived again, and a cheer ran along the shattered decks.

As the running-gear of the enemy was still intact, they easily kept out of the *Essex's* way, the *Phœbe* edged off, and, choosing her distance, kept up her tremendous firing. Putting his helm hard down, Captain Porter, finding the wind had shifted slightly, determined to run his ship on shore, land the crew, and blow her up. He approached once more within musket-shot of the sandy beach, when, in an instant, the wind shifted from the land, as if the British had bribed the elements, and once more the *Essex* was driving down upon the *Phœbe*. But her tiller-ropes were shot away, and the poor hulk was totally unmanageable.

At this moment one of the strangest incidents of the whole affair occurred.

Lieutenant Downes of the *Essex Junior*, which still lay at her old anchorage under the guns at the battery, loaded one of his boats and rowed through the fierce fusillade down to his superior officer. He came on board through a port, but his services could be of no avail. After a consultation, Porter ordered him to return to his own ship, and be prepared for defending her or destroying her in case of an attack. So Downes loaded his boat with wounded, and, leaving some of his crew on board the *Essex* to make room for them, he started to make his way back to his own little vessel. The enemy did not respect his cargo or his gallant action, but opened a hot fire upon him as he returned. Luckily, however, the small cutter escaped swamping, and the men at the long oars jumped her through the water at a rapid rate, despite the plashing of the bullets all around them.

Horrible now was the position of the American frigate. Her commander, in his desperation, persisted in the almost hopeless conflict, and succeeded, by bending a hawser to the sheet-anchor, in bringing his ship's head around; the few remaining guns of his broadside opened once more, and, strange to say, the *Phœbe*, which received this last and almost expiring effort, was beaten off; but the hawser parted, and with it failed the last hope of the *Essex*.

The flames that had started on her gun-deck and in her hold were bursting up the hatchways; a bundle of cartridges exploded, killing two men; and word was given out that the fire was near the magazine! Every boat was cut to pieces; it was three-quarters of a mile from shore.

Thinking that the ship might blow up at any moment, Porter gave orders to those who could swim to jump overboard and make for land.

The few remaining on board with the commander extinguished the fire. Porter immediately summoned a consultation of his officers, and was surprised to find that only one responded—Acting Lieutenant Stephen Decatur McKnight; the others were killed, or below, disabled by their wounds.

The late Admiral Farragut, who was a midshipman on board the *Essex*, had displayed wonderful courage throughout the engagement. He was one of the few midshipmen who were able to keep the deck.

Nothing could be done. The enemy in the smooth water had chosen their distance, and were firing by divisions in a deliberate, careful way, with coolness and accuracy. Almost every shot struck, and at twenty minutes past six Captain Porter, almost weeping from the excess of his grief, gave orders to strike the colors. It is probable that the enemy did not perceive his action; for ten minutes longer the terrible destruction continued; and once more, thinking that Hillyar was going to show no quarter, the brave American was about to hoist his flag again and fight until he sank, when the fire of the enemy suddenly ceased.

Thus ended one of the most bloody and obstinately contested actions in naval record. Out of the 255 men composing her crew, the *Essex* had but 151, including some of the wounded, able to stand on her decks; 58 were killed outright, 50 wounded, and 31 had been drowned.

The inhabitants of the city during the action had crowded to the shore. Their sympathies had been all with the American. When they had seen the various times when the *Essex* appeared to gain a slight advantage their cheers could be heard coming across the water. So close had the action been fought that many of the round shot from the *Phœbe's* guns had struck the land, and some of the spectators had been wounded.

When the first British officer boarded the captured vessel, so shocking was the sight that met his eyes that, used to scenes of carnage though he was, he staggered back and almost fainted, struck with the sickening horror.

The loss on the *Phœbe* and *Cherub* has never been ascertained, but it must have been severe. The former had received eighteen 12-pound shot below her water-line; her first lieutenant was killed, and her spars were badly wounded. It was with some difficulty that she had been kept afloat, but it was with more difficulty still that the *Essex* could be prevented from going to the bottom.

Captain Porter and his crew were paroled, and permitted to return to the United States in the *Essex Junior*, her armament having previously been taken out. When off New York Harbor they were overhauled by a razee frigate, the *Saturn*, of His Majesty's service, and the authority of the commander of the *Phœbe* to grant a passport to his prisoners was questioned.

All night the *Saturn* held the unarmed *Essex Junior* under her lee; but the next morning, taking advantage of a slight gray fog, Porter put off in his boat and rowed thirty miles to the shore, landing safely on Long Island.

To quote from the contemporaries again:

" His reception in the United States has been such as great service and distinguished valor deserve. The various interesting and romantic rumors that had reached this country concerning him during his cruise in the Pacific had excited the curiosity of the public to see this modern Sindbad; and, arriving in New York, his carriage was surrounded by the populace, who took out the horses and dragged him, with shouts and acclamations, to his lodgings."

The American commander's own account of the affair, which appears in a little volume entitled *Porter's Narrative*, shows well the spirit of this doughty old seaman, who, to use the expression applied to him, "had rather have fought than ate."

So virulent, however, were his tirades against the conduct of Captain Hillyar that it is only just to take into consideration that the latter commander, by refusing to take advantage of the many circumstances, would have missed entirely the object of his sailing from England; and his conduct has found many defenders among the writers of history on the other side of the water.

The honor rolls of the United States navy show the records of many a family history, and the name Porter has been associated with the service from the Revolution to the present day. The late Admiral David D. Porter was the younger son of the David Porter of *Essex* fame, and he had been named after his father, who was a doughty old sea-captain of the Revolution.

The second David Porter was born at Boston on the 1st of February, 1780. Thus he was but thirty-two years of age at the outbreak of the war with Great Britain, and his school of training had been the same as that of all the younger officers who now found themselves for the first time in command. He was with Bainbridge in the *Philadelphia* when that frigate was captured by the Tripolitans in 1803, and he suffered imprisonment with the rest of the officers during the time that Preble was endeavoring to liberate them. He had the honor of making the first capture of a regular navy vessel of the war, when, in July, the *Essex* compelled the *Alert*, of 20 guns, to lower her flag.

# XIII
## THE "PEACOCK" AND THE "EPERVIER"
[April 29th, 1814]

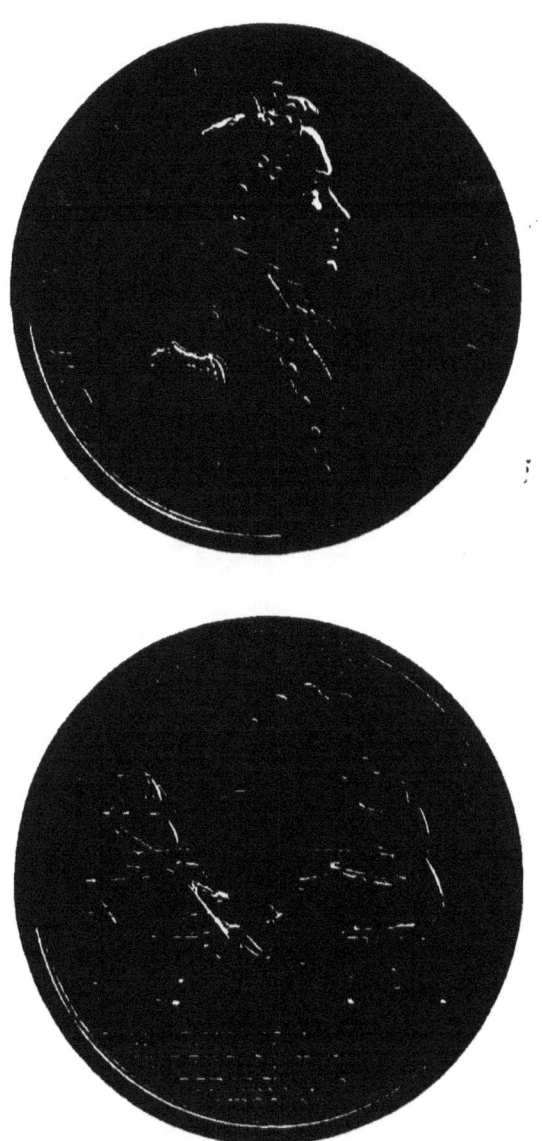

MEDAL PRESENTED BY CONGRESS TO
CAPTAIN LEWIS WARRINGTON

"CAPTAIN L. WARRINGTON, of Virginia, has been given the command of the *Peacock*, sloop of war of 18 guns. He expects soon to set sail and cruise to the southward in search of the enemy."

Such is the personal note appearing in that enterprising newspaper *The Register*, published in March, 1814.

The Captain Warrington referred to was but little known to the country at large, but those in a position of influence in the Navy Department must have discerned his worth and well estimated his valor, for they had given him command of the gallant little *Peacock*, of 18 guns (really mounting 22) and a crew of one hundred and sixty men.

In the middle of March he sailed from New York Harbor, and cruised, without events of much importance, along the Florida shore as far as Cape Canaveral. On the 29th of April, in latitude 27° 47' north and 80° 9' west longitude, the lookout spied three sails off to the windward. From the cut of the third, a brig, it was easy to mark her as a man-of-war.

Upon the appearance of the *Peacock* the merchantmen hauled their wind, and the brig bore away for the American. She gallantly commenced the action, and at no time showed a disposition to take advantage of being to windward and escaping with her consorts.

Neither vessel hailed, and there was little manœuvring. They began to fire at each other as soon as they were within range. In the beginning of the action the *Peacock* received two 32-pound shot in her fore-yard, and her head-sails were rendered almost useless. She was compelled to run at large; and again was proved, what no authority on the other side could ever deny, the infinitely superior gunnery that existed under the system in vogue in the American navy.

For a long time after the war there was much controversy concerning the weights of armament of the vessels engaged in single actions between this country and Great Britain. In this affair it is only just to say that the *Peacock* carried thirty-two more in her crew; the number of guns was exactly the same, but the *Peacock's* broadside was about one and one-quarter pounds heavier to the gun.

The action was continued for some time at close quarters, and once Captain Warrington drew off and hailed to ascertain whether his antagonist had struck, as her flag had been shot away.

On renewing the engagement the uselessness of continuing to fight was soon made apparent to the commander of the *Epervier*. She had received no less than forty-five shot in her hull, and had twenty-two men killed and wounded; the main-topmast was over her side. In fact, all her standing rigging and spars were injured, and five feet of water was already in her hold.

In hauling off to count up his injuries, Warrington discovered, to his delight, that not one round shot had reached his hull, that not one of his crew was killed, and only two were wounded. The effect of this news and the easy victory stimulated the Americans to tremendous exertion in trying to save the prize.

Upon boarding her it was discovered that she carried $118,000 in specie, and must have been a fine vessel when she commenced the action. With great difficulty the Americans succeeded in stopping some of the shot-holes beneath water, and turned all attention to caring for the prisoners and wounded, reeving new rigging and staying the tottering mainmast.

The prize had struck at 11 A.M. At sunset she was in a comparatively safe position, and sail could be made. To his sorrow, the American commander had found upon boarding the *Epervier* that three impressed American seamen by the names of Johnson, Peters, and Roberts had been killed. Often and often had it occurred that the impressed sailors for whom the United States had gone to war had been compelled to take up arms and serve the guns directed against the vessels of their own country. The anger at the news of these outrages must have done much to animate the seamen who sought to revenge them.

A contemporary speaks of the *Epervier* in this fashion: "She is one of the finest vessels of her class belonging to the enemy, built in 1812. She appears to have been one of their 'bragging vessels,' for it is said that when she left London bets were made that she would take an American sloop of war or small frigate." The odds must have been laid against events of that character thereafter.

Warrington determined to save the prize if possible, and placed her in command of Lieutenant J. B. Nicholson, with orders to proceed at once to Savannah. Knowing, however, that British vessels thronged the waters along the coast, Warrington determined to convoy his prize to port. He had hardly come within sight of land when two large frigates were discovered to the northward and leeward.

The *Peacock* spoke the *Epervier*, and, after some conversation, a plan was agreed on. They were abreast of Amelia Island, and the frigates were fast approaching and crowding on all sail.

Lieutenant Nicholson shouted to Captain Warrington to take off the crew from the *Epervier* and leave him and his sixteen men to handle her. Warrington complied, and endeavored to draw off the on-comers, it being his intention to try to slip into St. Mary's. Only one frigate fell to the ruse, and came about upon the *Peacock's* trail. The *Epervier*, which drew little water, kept well inshore, and under a light breeze made good headway. The wind, however, soon died to almost a calm, and the big vessel outside in the deeper water lowered her boats and manned them all, intending to cut out and retake the prize inshore. Fitful gusts of wind swept the captured vessel along, but during every pause the steady rowing of the British sailors brought the armed boats nearer. Suddenly they stopped all exertion, for Nicholson was shouting orders through his speaking-trumpet as if in command of one hundred men, instead of scarcely enough to haul his sheets and tacks. The ports dropped with a clatter and the boatswain's whistle rang out shrilly. The Englishmen were astounded; fearing that they had been drawn into a trap, turning tail, they scuttled out of range as quickly as possible and returned to the frigate. A breeze sprang up at this moment, and Nicholson was able to keep the *Epervier* on her course, and on the 1st of May the brig arrived safely in Savannah. Three days later the *Peacock* came in also.

Warrington's delight on seeing that his prize was safe was great, and he reported the *Epervier* in the following words: "She is one of their finest sloops of war, and is well calculated for our service. She sails extremely fast, and will require but little to send her to sea, as her armament and stores are complete."

In his letter to the Secretary of the Navy, when

at sea, on the night of the action, he speaks of his crew in this manly fashion: "Every officer, seaman, and marine did his duty, which is the highest compliment I can pay them."

The *Peacock* did not remain long inactive, but sailed for the Bay of Biscay and cruised along the coast of Portugal and among the islands. Time and again she was chased by English vessels, and was kept dodging from one position to another to avoid the many squadrons. It was not her luck to come across another vessel of war of anything like her size, but she captured handily fourteen sail of merchantmen.

The "commerce-destroyers" of those days were not spoken of in that term, but the trade of Great Britain was crippled severely by the swift-sailing privateers and our handy little sloops of war.

# XIV
## THE CRUISE OF THE "WASP"
[1814]

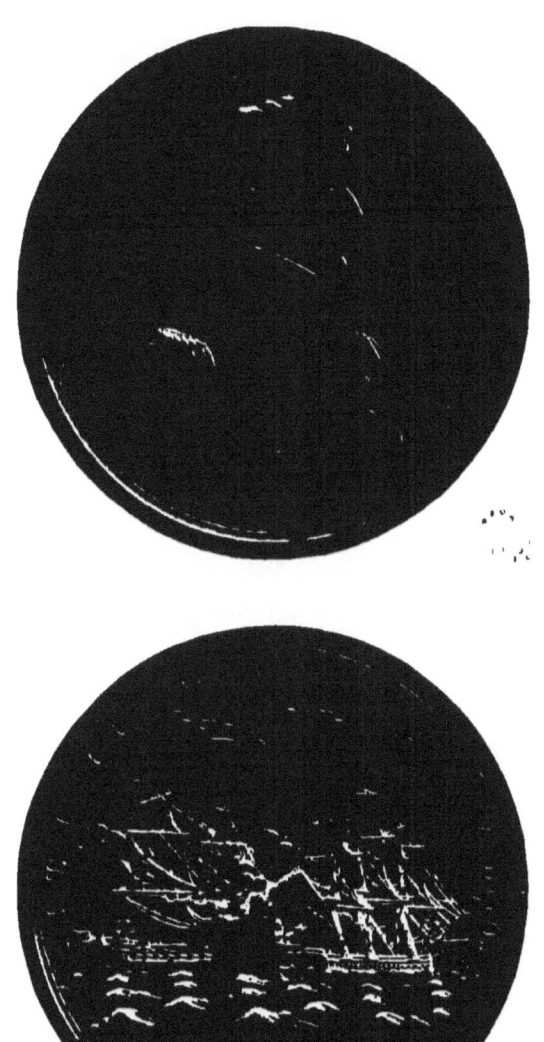

MEDAL PRESENTED BY CONGRESS TO
CAPTAIN JOHNSTON BLAKELEY

IN a very amusing cartoon, printed in the latter part of the year 1814 in an American paper, our cousin Johnnie Bull was represented flourishing a cutlass above his head and vainly endeavoring to defend himself from the attack of a nondescript-looking animal that had succeeded in running him through the body with its sting.

As was the custom in drawing cartoons at that time, the legend issued from the lips in a cloud, and Johnnie Bull appeared to be smoking out the words, "Save me, oh, save me from this vicious insect!"

The insect was supposed to be the United States sloop of war *Wasp*, of 18 guns, then on a most remarkable cruise in European waters. Under the command of Captain Johnston Blakeley her career had been smiled upon by good fortune.

In a cruise of under four months she had captured thirteen British merchantmen, and had engaged and caused to surrender two of the finest brigs in the service of Great Britain.

The value of her prizes was reckoned at not less than two hundred thousand pounds sterling.

On the 1st of May, 1814, the little sloop had set sail from Portsmouth, New Hampshire. She was manned by a crew of one hundred and seventy-three men, the majority of them being green hands, and many of them mere boys, for they averaged but twenty-three years in age.

Meeting with some severe weather when only a few days out, it is on record that one-third of her crew were sea-sick for a week. This fact, however, did not prevent them from becoming great fighters afterwards.

On the 28th of June, in latitude 48° 36′, longitude 11° 15′, she fell in with the *Reindeer*, sloop of war in His Majesty's service, mounting 19 guns—sixteen 24-pound carronades, two long 9-pounders, and a shifting 12-pounder. She had on board a complement of one hundred and eighteen men.

In an action that lasted but nineteen minutes from the first broadside, the *Reindeer* was destroyed, her ports having been blown into one gaping streak of splintered wood. Not a boat was left, and her foremast fell the day after the action.

As it was found impossible to take her into port, the prisoners were removed from the *Reindeer* and she was set on fire. That she had been gallantly defended is evident from the reports of the action. William Manners, her commander, a brave, fearless man, was killed, and twenty-three officers and seamen with him. The first lieutenant and the master were severely wounded, and forty seamen were on the list also.

The *Wasp* lost five killed and twenty-one wounded. She was but slightly hurt, and within a few hours of the action could have commenced another.

Wishing to get rid of his prisoners as soon as possible, Captain Blakeley overhauled a Portuguese brig, placed them on board of her, and sent them to England.

No doubt the *Wasp* was one of the finest sailing craft of her day. Her lines are spoken of as being remarkably fine; and one of her officers writes, in a private letter, as follows:

"The *Wasp* is a beautiful ship, and the finest sea boat, I believe, in the world. Our officers and crew are young and ambitious. They fight with more cheerfulness than they do any other duty. Captain Blakeley is a brave and discreet officer, as cool and collected in action as at table."

In those old days of sailing, given the weather-gage and the breeze that suited her best qualities, a handy vessel could boldly sail into view of a powerful fleet of the enemy, and she could actually present the tableau of an agile wolf following at the heels of a very angry herd of bulls, any one of which could toss her into the air or grind her under foot. So spry a sailer was the *Wasp* that she could slip away from even a towering seventy-four, given her best weather.

After a protracted and tedious stay in L'Orient, the little sloop made her way to sea on the 27th of August. On the 30th she captured the British brig *Lettice*, and on the next day the British brig *Bon Accord*.

The morning of the 1st of September dawned bright and clear. There was just the breeze that enabled the *Wasp* to show her finest form. Very early the lookout discovered a fleet of ten sail to the windward, away in advance. Plunging up and down lazily, scarcely moving in the light breeze, was a huge line-of-battle ship, and close to her was a bomb vessel.

The Yankee captain audaciously came down before the wind. In full sight of H. M. S. *Armada*, the seventy-four, and the other armed consort, Blakeley cut out the brig *Mary*. She was laden with brass and iron cannon and military stores from Gibraltar to England. As she was a slow sailer she was set on fire, after the prisoners had been removed.

Endeavor was made to take another of the convoy. The consternation and rage of the commander of the ship of line can well be imagined. There was not breeze enough for his great vessel to make headway by tacking, but the wind, changing a few points, enabled him to creep down towards the American, whereupon Blakeley swung about leisurely, and soon left the ponderous Englishman hull down.

When he had shaken off his pursuer he resumed his course, and at half-past six in the evening sighted four vessels at almost the same moment; two were to starboard and two off the larboard bow, the latter being farthest to windward. He picked out the nearest, a brig, and set all sail to come within gunshot of her.

At seven the chase commenced making signals with flags, and soon after with lanterns and rockets. It was past nine o'clock and quite dark when the *Wasp* came up within hailing distance. To quote from a British account of the affair, dated Cork, September 7th: "The Englishman spoke first, and demanded to know who the silent on-comer was. The 'Yankee,' in reply," says the account, "called through his trumpet, 'Heave to, and I'll let you know who I am.' At the same time a gun was fired by the *Avon*, and the most sanguinary action commenced, which continued until eleven o'clock, when the American sheared off and said, 'This is the *Wasp*.'" Then the British account, for some reason, adds: "She appeared to be in a sinking state and glad to get away."

In Captain Blakeley's letter to the Secretary of the Navy he mentions circumstances which may throw some light upon the actual happenings. After an hour's sharp interchange of broadsides it was imagined that the *Avon* had struck, and orders were given to cease firing. Blakeley hailed, but received no answer. Suddenly the Britisher opened up with his guns again. It was twelve minutes past ten when he was hailed the second time. The enemy had suffered greatly, and had made no return to his last two broadsides. A cutter was lowered away, and as it was leaving the side of the *Wasp* to board the prize a second brig was discovered a little distance astern standing down before the freshening breeze.

The crew were again sent to quarters, and everything was made ready for another action. A few minutes later the two other sail which had been off to windward were discovered also coming down towards the *Wasp*. The braces of the latter had been shot away, and it was necessary to keep off the wind until others might be rove. Blakeley did not endeavor to hasten. It was his intention to draw the second and foremost brig away from her companions and engage her as soon as they had reached a good distance from the others. To his surprise, however, the brig, which, from the English account, we make out to be the *Castilian*, hauled her wind as soon as she came within range, fired one broadside, and retraced her course to join her consorts, who were gathered about the *Avon*.

To Blakeley's disappointment, he had to give up taking the prize, whose name and forces he did not know, as it had been impossible to distinguish the answer to his first hail.

The *Wasp* was struck by four shot in the hull, each of which shot was thirty-two pounds in weight, being one and three-quarter pounds heavier than any the American carried.

For a long time the fate of the vessel which she had been fighting was not known, but she sank a few hours after the action. The loss on board the *Wasp* was two killed and one wounded. From the English account, the loss on board the *Avon* was nine killed and thirty-three wounded. As she was

THE "WASP'S" FIGHT WITH THE "AVON."

sinking, the *Tartarus*, a sloop of war, came up and took on board forty of her crew.

In the list of the vessels of the American navy in commission during the war of 1812 the name of the *Wasp* is starred, with one or two others bearing the same mark, and, looking at the bottom of the page, we see this short comment, "Lost at sea." This was the sad fate of the gallant little craft which caused John Bull so much trouble in her short career. It was never known what became of her. Some authorities on the British side stated that she had sunk from the injuries received in her action with the *Avon;* but of course we have the report of Captain Blakeley sent by a vessel spoken off the Western Isles.

In speaking of the disappearance a contemporary writes: "The most general impression is that she [the *Wasp*] was lost by one of those casualties incident to the great deep which have destroyed so many gallant vessels in a manner no one knows how."

A strange circumstance, however, gives rise to a supposition. A British frigate put into Lisbon in a shattered condition. She reported having fallen in with a vessel and having engaged her through the better part of the night. She had made out that her antagonist was much smaller than herself, and evidently an American. She had not surrendered, and had disappeared suddenly, "as if the sea had swallowed her." This may have been the *Wasp*.

The fact remains, however, that no trace of her or any of her crew was ever found after she spoke the vessel at the Western Isles. The first *Wasp*, captured with her prize (the British sloop *Frolic*) by an English ship of the line, was also lost at sea, after being refitted and commissioned in the English service.

Johnston Blakeley was an Irish-American. He was born in Ireland (in the village of Seaford, in the county of Down). When he was but two years old his father, John Blakeley, emigrated to America and took up his residence in Philadelphia, from whence he moved to the South. He had the misfortune to lose all of his children with the exception of Johnston, whom he sent to New York for his education. This was in the year 1790; but the young man, although he studied law with the intention of becoming a member of the bar, gave up all idea of it shortly after his father's death. He left the University of North Carolina, at which he was a student, and succeeded in getting a midshipman's warrant when he was nineteen years of age, much older than the average run of reefers.

Blakeley was a favorite with all who knew him, and his loss was mourned by all his countrymen.

# XV
# THE BATTLE OF LAKE CHAMPLAIN
[September 11th, 1814]

MEDAL PRESENTED BY CONGRESS TO
CAPTAIN THOMAS MACDONOUGH

THE first Thomas Macdonough was a major in the Continental army, and his three sons also possessed desires for entering the service of their country. The oldest had been a midshipman under Commodore Truxton, but being wounded in the action between the *Constellation* and *L'Insurgent*, he had to retire from the navy owing to the amputation of his leg. But his younger brother, Thomas Macdonough, Jr., succeeded him, and he has rendered his name and that of Lake Champlain inseparable; but his fearlessness and bravery were shown on many occasions long before he was ordered to the lakes.

In 1806 he was first lieutenant of the *Siren*, a little sloop of war in the Mediterranean service. On one occasion when Captain Smith, the commander of the *Siren*, had gone on shore, young Lieutenant Macdonough saw a boat from a British frigate lying in the harbor row up to an American brig a short distance off, and afterwards put out again with one more man in her than she had originally. This looked suspicious, and Macdonough sent to the brig to ascertain the reason, with the result that he found that an American had been impressed by the English captain's orders. Macdonough quietly lowered his own boat, and put after the heavy cutter, which he soon overhauled. Although he had but four men with him, he took the man out of the cutter and brought him on board the *Siren*. When the English captain heard, or rather saw, what had occurred — it was right under the bow of his frigate that the affair took place—he waxed wroth, and, calling away his gig, he rowed to the *Siren* to demand an explanation.

The following account of the incident is quoted from the life of Macdonough in Frost's *Naval Biography*:

"The Englishman desired to know how Macdonough dared to take a man from one of His Majesty's boats. The lieutenant, with great politeness, asked him down into the cabin; this he refused, at the same time repeating the same demand, with abundance of threats. The Englishman threw out some threats that he would take the man by force, and said he would haul the frigate alongside the *Siren* for that purpose. To this Macdonough replied that he supposed his ship could sink the *Siren*, but as long as she could swim he should keep the man. The English captain said to Macdonough:

"'You are a very young man, and a very indiscreet young man. Suppose I had been in the boat—what would you have done?'

"'I would have taken the man or lost my life.'

"'What, sir! would you attempt to stop me, if

I were now to attempt to impress men from that brig?'

"'I would; and to convince yourself I would, you have only to make the attempt.'

"On this the Englishman went on board his ship, and shortly afterwards was seen bearing down in her in the direction of the American vessel. Macdonough ordered his boat manned and armed, got into her himself, and was in readiness for pursuit. The Englishman took a circuit around the American brig, and returned again to the frigate. When Captain Smith came on board he justified the conduct of Macdonough, and declared his intention to protect the American seaman."

Although Macdonough was very young, and his rank but that of a lieutenant, people who knew him were not surprised to hear that he had been appointed to take command of the little squadron on Lake Champlain. These vessels were built of green pine, and almost without exception constructed in a hurried fashion. They had to be of light draught, and yet, odd to relate, their general model was the same as that of ships that were expected to meet storms and high seas.

Macdonough was just the man for the place; as in the case of Perry, he had a superb self-reliance and was eager to meet the enemy.

Lake Champlain and the country that surrounds it were considered of great importance by the English, and, descending from Canada, large bodies of troops poured into New York State. But the American government had, long before the war was fairly started, recognized the advantage of keeping the water communications on the northern frontier. The English began to build vessels on the upper part of the lake, and the small force of ships belonging to the Americans was increased as fast as possible. It was a race to see which could prepare the better fleet in the shorter space of time.

In the fall of the year 1814 the English had one fairly sized frigate, the *Confiance*, mounting 39 guns; a brig, the *Linnet;* a sloop, *Chubb*, and the sloop *Finch;* besides which they possessed thirteen large galleys, aggregating 18 guns. In all, therefore, the English fleet mounted 95 guns. The Americans had the *Saratoga*, sloop of war, 26 guns; the *Eagle*, 20; the *Ticonderoga*, 17; the *Preble*, 7; and ten galleys carrying 16; their total armament was nine guns less than the British.

By the first week in September, Sir George Prevost had organized his forces, and started at the head of fourteen thousand men to the southward. It was his intention to dislodge General Macomb, who was stationed at Plattsburg, where considerable fortifications had been erected. A great deal of the militia force had been drawn down the State to the city of New York, owing to the fears then entertained that the British intended making an attack upon the city from their fleet. It was Sir George's plan to destroy forever the power of the Americans upon the lake, and for that reason it was necessary to capture the naval force which had been for some time under the command of Macdonough. The English leader arranged a plan with Captain Downie, who was at the head of the squadron, that simultaneous attacks should be made by water and land. At eight o'clock on the morning of September 11th news was brought to Lieutenant Macdonough that the enemy was approaching. As his own vessels were in a good position to repel an attack, he decided to remain at anchor, and await the onslaught in a line formation. In about an hour the enemy had come within gunshot distance, and formed a line of his own parallel with that of the Americans. There was little or no breeze, and consequently small chance for manœuvring. The *Confiance* evidently claimed the honor of exchanging broadsides with the *Saratoga*. The *Linnet* stopped opposite the *Eagle*, and the galleys rowed in and began to fire at the *Ticonderoga* and the *Preble*.

Macdonough wrote such a clear and concise account of the action that it is best to quote from it:

" . . . The whole force on both sides became engaged, the *Saratoga* suffering much from the heavy fire of the *Confiance*. I could perceive at the same time, however, that our fire was very destructive to her. The *Ticonderoga*, Lieutenant-Commandant Cassin, gallantly sustained her full share of the action. At half-past ten the *Eagle*, not being able to bring her guns to bear, cut her cable, and anchored in a more eligible position, between my ship and the *Ticonderoga*, where she very much annoyed the enemy, but unfortunately leaving me exposed to a galling fire from the enemy's brig.

"Our guns on the starboard side being nearly all dismounted or unmanageable, a stern-anchor was let go, the bower-cable cut, and the ship winded with a fresh broadside on the enemy's ship, which soon after surrendered. Our broadside was then sprung to bear on the brig, which struck about fifteen minutes afterwards. The sloop which was opposed to the *Eagle* had struck some time before, and drifted down the line. The sloop which was with their galleys had also struck. Three of their galleys are said to be sunk; the others pulled off. Our galleys were about obeying with alacrity the signal to follow them, when all the vessels were reported to me to be in a sinking state. It then became necessary to annul the signal to the galleys, and order their men to the pumps. I could only look at the enemy's galleys going off in a shattered condition; for there was not a mast in either squadron that could stand to make sail on. The lower rigging, being nearly all shot away, hung down as though it had just been placed over the mastheads.

"The *Saratoga* had fifty-nine round shot in her hull; the *Confiance* one hundred and five. The enemy's shot passed principally just over our heads, as there were not twenty whole hammocks in the nettings at the close of the action, which lasted, without intermission, two hours and twenty minutes.

"The absence and sickness of Lieutenant Raymond Perry left me without the assistance of that able officer. Much ought fairly to be attributed to him for his great care and attention in disciplining the ship's crew, as her first lieutenant. His place was filled by a gallant young officer, Lieutenant Peter Gamble, who, I regret to inform you, was killed early in the action."

The English had begun the action as if they never doubted the result being to their advantage, and before taking up their positions in the line parallel to Macdonough's, Downie had sailed upon the waiting fleet bows on; thus most of his vessels had been severely raked before they were able to return the fire. As soon as Sir George Prevost saw the results of the action out on the water, he gave up all idea of conquest, and began the retreat that left New York free to breathe again. The frontier was saved. The hills and the shores of the lake had been crowded with multitudes of farmers, and the two armies encamped on shore had stopped their own preparations and fighting to watch.

Sir George Prevost had bombarded the American forts from the opposite side of the River Saranac, and a brigade endeavored to ford the river with the intention of attacking the rear of General Macomb's position. However, they got lost in the woods, and were recalled by a mounted messenger just in time to hear the cheers and shouts of victory arise from all about them.

In the battle the *Saratoga* had twenty-eight men killed and twenty-nine wounded, more than a quarter of her entire crew; the *Eagle* lost thirteen killed and twenty wounded; the *Ticonderoga*, six killed and six wounded; the *Preble*, two killed; and the galleys, three killed and three wounded. The *Saratoga* was hulled fifty-five times, and had caught on fire twice from the hot shot fired by the *Confiance*. The latter vessel was reported to have lost forty-one killed outright and eighty-three wounded. In all, the British loss was eighty-four killed and one hundred and ten wounded.

Macdonough received substantial testimonials of gratitude from the country at large, the Legislature of New York giving him one thousand acres of land and the State of Vermont two hundred. Besides this, the corporations of Albany and New York City made him the present of a valuable lot, and from his old command in the Mediterranean he received a handsome presentation sword.

# XVI
## THE LOSS OF THE "PRESIDENT"
[January 15th, 1815]

IN recording the actions of the war of 1812 that gave lustre to our navy and added to the records of its heroes, we have already included two in which the results were defeat and capture of American ships. The *Essex* and the *Chesapeake* are here referred to, the latter being the only case in which the opposing forces approached an equality. There is one other action still to be touched upon, which, though disastrous, cannot but reflect honor upon those connected with it.

Stephen Decatur, the idol of the American service, had been given the command of the frigate *President*, which had been refitting in the harbor of New York.

On the evening of the 14th of January, 1815, he sailed into the lower bay, intending to make his way to sea under cover of the night, as it was known that a heavy squadron of the English had been hovering along the coasts of New Jersey and Long Island.

In leaving the harbor near Sandy Hook, owing to some mistake of the pilot, the *President* grounded heavily on a sand-bar, and for an hour and a half she struck continually in her efforts to escape, breaking several of her rudder-braces and straining her seams so badly that she commenced to leak very fast. Decatur determined to return to the harbor, as he suspected, what was afterwards proved to be true, that the *President* had carried away part of her false keel, and was badly hogged (*i. e.*, broken and bent near her keelson). Owing to a strong wind rising, it was found impossible to put the *President* about, and the tide being at the flood, it became necessary to force her over the bar at all hazards. By ten o'clock that night she had succeeded in freeing herself, and shaped her course along the shore of Long Island, steering southeast by east.

Shortly after daybreak three ships were discovered ahead. The *President* hauled her wind and passed two miles to the northward of them. As the morning mist disappeared, it was discovered that four ships were in chase—one on each quarter and two astern. The leading ship, from the height of her towering masts, was made out to be a razee. She commenced firing, but at such a distance that the shot fell short.

At twelve the steady breeze which had been blowing became light and baffling. The *President*, despite her crippled condition, had left the large vessel far behind, but the next ship astern was proving herself a faster sailer, and was gradually gaining— creeping up with every puff of wind. The *President* sat deep in the water, and plunged downward into the sea as if she had been waterlogged. Immediately all hands were occupied in lightening the ship, starting the water in the butts, cutting away the anchors, throwing overboard provisions, cables, spare boats, and every article to be gotten at, while the men aloft were hoisting buckets and keeping the sails wet from the royals down.

At three o'clock the large ship, which had been joined by a brig, came up rapidly. It was the *Endymion*, mounting 50 guns, and she commenced to fire as she neared with her forward battery, while Decatur replied with his stern-chasers. Thus it continued for two hours, when the Englishman obtained a position on the starboard quarter at less than point-blank range, and maintained it so cleverly that neither the *President's* stern nor quarter guns would bear. For half an hour the vessels sailed on, firing occasional guns, and keeping back their broadsides, the Englishman wishing, no doubt, to capture the *President* without crippling her, while Decatur hoped to be able to close, as he had had his boarders waiting for some time. It became evident, however, that the Englishman did not wish close quarters; and as it was growing dusk, Decatur made up his mind to alter his course farther to the south, for the purpose of bringing the enemy abeam. Meanwhile the ships astern were approaching, and would soon be within range. For two hours and a half longer the Englishman and the *President* sailed side by side, and the action gave cause for some pretty writing and press controversy afterwards, as all unfinished international contests will.

However, there is no question whatever that the *President* during the running fight completely disabled her antagonist, and at last left her drifting round and round helplessly before eight o'clock had passed.

It was growing dark, but the other ships of the squadron could be made out by their signal-lights, and to lower a boat to take possession of the *Endymion* was impossible. One more attempt Decatur made to avoid capture, and to accomplish this he sailed close to the *Endymion* and exposed himself to a raking fire, being within range for over half an hour, but not a shot was heard. The Englishman had been placed entirely out of the combat.

At eleven it had lightened considerably, and two fresh ships of the enemy had crawled up within gunshot. They were the *Pomone* and the *Tenedos*, heavy frigates. When within musket-shot the *Pomone* opened fire on the larboard bow, and the *Tenedos* swung across the *President's* wake, taking a raking position on her quarter.

With a breaking heart the gallant Decatur saw that there was nothing for it but surrender. One-fifth of his crew had been killed or wounded, the ship was crippled aloft and leaking badly, and he hauled down his flag.

The joy of the English officers when they found who it was that had yielded to them was great, and it must be recorded that they did everything in their power to make it comfortable for the wound-

THE "PRESIDENT" ENDEAVORING TO ESCAPE

ed, and that their treatment of the officers was courteous and kindly. For twenty-four hours after the action it fell a dead calm, and the crews of the squadron were kept occupied in repairing the crippled ships. As if to enforce the idea that the *Endymion* had not surrendered, Decatur was placed on board of her, a cabin prisoner.

On the 17th a tremendous gale came from the eastward, which played havoc with the late combatants, the *President's* masts going by the board, and the *Endymion* losing her bowsprit, fore and main mast, and mizzen-topmast, being compelled to throw overboard all her upper-deck guns. It had been impossible for Decatur to ascertain the exact number of the killed and wounded, but he speaks of his great sorrow at the loss of three of his most trusted lieutenants — Babbit, Howell, and Hamilton, the last being the son of the late Secretary of the Navy. It was he who had had the honor of conveying the news of the capture of the *Macedonian* to Washington, and who had appeared, as we have recorded, at the ball given by Dolly Madison wrapped in the colors of the captured ship.

Decatur and his officers were given the freedom of the island of Bermuda, and crowds swarmed to visit the captured *President* as she lay decked with British flags in the harbor.

Captain Hays of the *Majestic*, to whom Decatur had surrendered his sword, returned it at once, and proved to be a friend who was worth the gaining.

Upon the investigation of the action Decatur was honorably exonerated, and Alexander Murray, the President of the Court of Inquiry, expressed himself in the following words:

"We consider the management of the *President* from the time the chase commenced until her surrender as the highest evidence of the experience, skill, and resources of her commander, and of the ability and seamanship of her officers and crew. We fear that we cannot express in a manner that will do justice to our feelings our admiration of the conduct of Commodore Decatur and of all under his command.... In this unequal conflict the enemy gained a ship, but the victory was ours."

Referring to the press comments at the time, a very interesting circumstance occurred, which may prove to be well worth the reading, especially as showing that contemporaneous press notices taking only one view of a question are untrustworthy recorders of history. A Bermuda paper, the *Royal Gazette*, published on the 2d of April a scurrilous and unwarrantable attack, false in its every statement, that impugned the character of Decatur and cast a slur on the name of each one of his officers. The article, in giving the reports of the capture, stated that the *President* had *struck* to the *Endymion*, and that after she had done so Commodore Decatur concealed sixty-eight men in the hold of the *President* for the purpose of rising on the prize crew and recapturing her. On the appearance of this account

Captain Hope of the *Endymion* immediately sent an officer to Commodore Decatur, disclaiming any participation in the article, and the governor of the island demanded of the editor of the *Royal Gazette* that he should immediately retract the statement. This the editor, much against his will, did, but inserted a foot-note in large print stating that the retraction was inserted "merely as an act of generosity and a palliative for the irritated feelings of prisoners of war." He asserted that what he had said at first was correct, and declared that the deception he had referred to was planned and authorized by Commodore Decatur. It is of interest to quote an extract from an official letter sent by the Governor and Commander-in-Chief of Bermuda to the editor of the *Royal Gazette* upon the appearance of this second article.

The governor's secretary writes for his chief as follows:

" *The Editor of the Royal Gazette:*

"Your publication of Thursday imposes it upon His Excellency the Governor, as a duty to himself, to Captain Hope, and to the British nation, and in common justice to Commodore Decatur, who is not present to defend himself from the aspersions that you have cast upon him, not to admit of such a document standing uncontradicted in a paper published under the immediate authority of His Majesty's government. His Excellency is thoroughly aware of the great importance of preserving to the utmost extent perfect freedom of discussion and the fullest liberty of the press in every part of the British dominions. Undoubtedly, therefore, nothing could be further from his intentions than the most distant desire to compel a British editor to retract a statement founded on truth;

but when a statement is founded on falsehood, His Excellency conceives it to be incumbent on him equally, in duty to the British public and in support of the true character of the British press, to demand that that falsehood, whether directed against friend or foe, should be instantly retracted, or that the paper which thinks fit to disgrace its columns by persevering in error should no longer be distinguished by royal protection."

Some weeks later, in an issue of March 2d, the following extract attracts attention in a Bermuda journal:

"On Wednesday evening last Mr. Randolph, of the United States Navy, late of the *President* frigate, in company with some other officers of the ship, attacked the editor of the *Royal Gazette* in a most violent and unprovoked manner with a stick, while he was walking unarmed. The timely arrival of some British officers prevented his proceeding to further acts of violence, and, the guard shortly after coming up, the officer decamped, and the next morning, we understand, he was hoisted into a boat at the crane from the Market Wharf and absconded. An honorable way, truly, for an officer to quit a place where he had been treated with civility and politeness."

However, it will not do to leave the subject without quoting from a letter which the Mr. Randolph referred to wrote over his own signature and sent to the editors of the *Commercial Advertiser*, after his return to New York, in which he observes, after reference to the Bermuda *Royal Gazette*, the affair of the stick, and the "acts of violence," as follows:

"As soon as I read the scurrilous remarks in the *Royal Gazette* of the fifteenth ult., in relation to the capture of the late U. S. frigate *President*, I walked to the King's Square with the determination to chastise the editor. I soon fell in with him, and executed my purpose in the most ample and satisfactory manner. There was no

American officer in the company except Midshipman Emmett, and Mr. Ward, the editor, was accompanied by Lieutenant Sammon, of the Royal Navy, but by neither of these officers was I interrupted or assisted in the operation.

"Having previously obtained my passports, and being advised that the editor of the *Royal Gazette* was taking measures to employ the civil authority against me, I left the island the next day, for the United States.

"I am, Gentlemen, etc., etc.,
"R. B. RANDOLPH, Midshipman,
"Late of the U. S. frigate *President*."

Upon Decatur's return to the United States he was treated as a hero, and received the usual ovation given to victors when they return to their native land. The *President* was spoken of by her captors as a model of naval architecture, and her method of construction recommended to British ship-builders.

# XVII

## THE "CONSTITUTION," THE "CYANE," AND THE "LEVANT"

[February 20th, 1815]

MEDAL PRESENTED BY CONGRESS TO
CAPTAIN CHARLES STEWART

CHARLES STEWART was a Philadelphian. He was born on the 28th day of July, 1778, shortly after the evacuation of the city by the British. His mother was left a widow when he was but two years old. Overcoming many hardships, Mrs. Stewart managed to support herself and her large family of eight children during the troublous times of the Revolution. At the age of thirteen Charles entered the merchant service as a cabin-boy, and speedily began to show that he had in him the material for making an officer.

At the age of twenty he was in command of a vessel in the Indian trade, but shortly after he attained this rank he accepted a commission as lieutenant in the navy of the United States. Stewart's able handling of the little schooner *Experiment*, of 12 guns, on several occasions brought him to the attention of the country, and his conduct in the Mediterranean won for him the praise of his superiors and the admiration of the service. He was a fine-looking, energetic man, who possessed a manner that is said to have been most fascinating; but, like all of his school, he was above everything else a fighting man.

In the fall of the year 1814, after the repulse of

the British at Norfolk, Captain Stewart, who at the beginning of the war had been in command of the 36-gun frigate *Constellation*, was given the post then most desired above all others in our navy—that of commander of "Old Ironsides."

After undergoing some repairs in the navy-yard, the *Constitution*, with a veteran crew, sailed from the port of Boston and proceeded southward. For some time she hung about the Bermudas, waiting in vain for an encounter; thence she sailed away for the coasts of Surinam, Berbice, and Demerara; cruised to windward of the island of Barbadoes, St. Vincent, Martinique, off St. Kitt's, St. Eustatius, Porto Rico, and Santa Cruz, and succeeded in capturing and destroying the *Picton*, of 16 guns; a merchant ship of 10 guns; the brig *Catherine*, 10 guns; and an armed schooner, the *Phœnix*. But no foe was seen that was worthy of her mettle, and it appeared that bad luck was in the breezes.

At this time the *Constitution* must have presented a peculiar appearance while under way; her sails were the same she had carried in her cruises under Hull and Bainbridge, and the shot-holes made by the *Guerrière* and the *Java* were plain to view, like the honorable scars of a veteran. Patched and threadbare, her canvas was in no condition to stand a blow or to hold the wind. In those days the *Constitution* was a marked vessel in many senses. In view of the reputation she had earned, there were no frigates of her class that appeared to seek her out, and it was not considered a disgrace to avoid a meeting with "the dangerous nondescript," as the British press had labelled her. If the fact was once ascertained what vessel it was that carried that high freeboard and those brown patched sails, His Majesty's commanders generally showed a tenderness that their reputations would hardly lead one to expect. In the Mona Passage, for instance, Captain Stewart chased, but failed to come up with, the British frigate *La Pique*, and on two separate occasions he tried to entice the enemy to meet him by unfurling at first sight the enormous flag that also distinguished the *Constitution* above the other frigates in our service, but all to no purpose; and in March Stewart determined to return to the United States in order to refit completely. But he was not to reach home without an adventure.

Probably no vessel in the world had so many narrow escapes from capture as had the *Constitution*; only masterly seamanship had kept her from being taken.

From 1813 to the close of the war the English frigates generally cruised in pairs; and off the New England coast, on her return voyage, the *Constitution* ran across the *Junon* and *La Nymphe*, each of 50 guns. She managed to outsail them by a narrow margin, and arrived safely at Marblehead in the latter part of April. She rested in Massachusetts Bay for seven months, completely refitting under the eye of Captain Stewart himself; and in December she again proceeded to sea, and was then, beyond doubt, the best equipped and best ordered vessel of her class that ever answered helm.

Stewart shaped his course for his favorite cruising-ground, the high seas to the eastward of the Bermudas, and on the 24th of the month he captured the English brig *Lord Nelson*, and took the ship *Susan* with a valuable cargo, sending the latter to New York. Then he bore away east, with the intention of reaching the waters in the neighborhood of the Madeira Islands.

The morning of the 20th of February began with light breezes from the east and cloudy weather. At 1 P.M. a sail was discovered two points off the larboard and three leagues or more away. The *Constitution* bore up at once, and made all sail in chase. In half an hour the stranger was seen to be a ship, and in a few minutes another vessel was made out ahead; both were close-hauled, and about ten miles apart. At four o'clock it was seen that the weathermost ship was signalling her consort, who immediately shortened sail and waited for her.

For an hour the three vessels sailed on. The two strangers, that were closing on each other gradually, displayed no flags; and although at too great a distance to reach the nearer vessel, Stewart commenced to fire with his bow guns, in the hope that they would display their colors; but to no purpose. It was not doubted, however, that they were English, and the *Constitution* cleared for action. Soon they passed within hail of one another, and, hauling by the wind on the starboard tack, showed that they were prepared to fight.

Now commenced the usual struggle for the advantage of the weather-gage; but, finding that the *Constitution* could outpoint them, the British vessels gave up the attempt, and, forming in line about half a cable's length apart, awaited her on-coming, shortening sail, and evidently preparing some concerted method of attack. At six Stewart shook out his tremendous flag, and the British ensigns climbed up in answer; at the same moment both vessels gave three rousing cheers. But in grim silence the *Constitution* bore down upon them, ranged up on the starboard side of the sternmost, and let go her broadside at a distance of only three hundred yards. The English replied with spirit, and the cannonading became furious. There being little wind, a great bank of sulphurous smoke, impenetrable as any fog, settled over the water on the *Constitution's* lee, and completely hid her antagonists. For three minutes the *Constitution* ceased her fire altogether (the enemy having slackened also), and then Stewart descried the topmasts of the leader stretching above the rolling clouds abreast of him. He fired his broadside, and again the smoke swallowed her from sight, just as it was seen that the ship astern had luffed to take up a raking position on the larboard quarter. The superior seamanship of the American tars and the quality of the vessel they manned could not be shown better than by the manœuvre which followed. Stewart braced aback his main and mizzen topsails, and immediately the *Constitution* gathered sternway and slid backwards through the smoke. What must have been the astonishment of Captain Gordon Falcon, the British commander, when he saw alongside of him the enemy that he had hoped, a few minutes before, to take at such a disadvantage! The foremost vessel, that had received the previous broadside of the *Constitution*, kept pegging away at a spectre in the sulphurous cloud.

At thirty-five minutes past six the enemy's fire again slackened, and the headmost ship was discovered bearing up. Now the *Constitution* reversed her tactics, shot ahead, crossed the first vessel's stern and raked her fearfully, sailed about the sternmost and raked her also; then, ranging up within hail on the larboard quarter, she prepared for another broadside, when the last ship fired a lee gun and remained silent. At ten minutes of seven Stewart lowered his boat and took possession of His Majesty's ship *Cyane*, mounting 34 guns, commanded by Captain Gordon Falcon. The moon had risen by this time; the smoke had cleared away, and it was seen that the other ship was trying her best to get away to a place of safety. Seeing this, at once the *Constitution* spread all sail in chase, and gallantly the smaller vessel, finding escape impossible, stood back close-hauled to meet her. They crossed on opposite tacks, and the *Constitution* wore immediately under the enemy's stern and raked her with a broadside.

Again the Englishman spread all sail, and endeavored to escape by running free. The *Constitution* broke out her lighter sail in chase, firing well-directed shots from her starboard bow-chaser. At ten, seeing she could not escape, the English vessel fired a gun, struck her colors, and yielded.

She proved to be His Majesty's ship the *Levant*, mounting 21 guns, Captain George Douglass.

Before midnight Stewart had manned both his prizes, repaired his rigging, shifted his sails, and had his vessel in as good condition as before the encounter.

The *Cyane* was a ship that had made a reputation for herself in the war with France. She was one of the crack sloops of war in the English service. Only a year before she had engaged a French 44-gun frigate, and kept her at bay until help came in the shape of a seventy-four. Her commander was so crestfallen at having to surrender that when he came aboard a prisoner he hardly recognized Stewart's courteous greetings and compliments.

Down in the cabin of the *Constitution* a little scene was enacted that must have been dramatic. Captain Douglass and Captain Falcon were treated as honored guests by Captain Stewart, and over their wine at dinner the day after the capture the two Englishmen indulged in a dispute, each placing the responsibility for the defeat upon the other's shoulders.

Stewart listened without comment for some minutes, and then rising, gravely said, "Gentlemen, there is only one way that I see to decide this question — to put you both on your ships again, give you back your crews, and try it over."

Either the humor or the force of this remark must have struck each one of his late antagonists, for they ceased their bickering at once.

An anecdote is related showing the spirit of the men on board the *Constitution* at the time. As she forged down upon the waiting English vessels grog was issued, as was customary, to the crews standing at the guns. An old quartermaster, noting with anger the eagerness of the men to claim a double share, as there were two vessels to fight, walked down the deck and kicked over two buckets of the spirits into the scuppers, exclaiming, "Shame, messmates; we need no Dutch courage on board this ship!"

This little incident, while it might not have dampened the crew's ardor, may have accounted for the lack of cheers.

It is to be noticed that the weight of shot fired by the British vessels was heavier than the *Constitution's* by ninety pounds.

In the action with the *Guerrière* the *Constitution* had been hulled three times, and in that with the *Java* four times. In this engagement thirteen shots reached her hull.

Only one of the prizes was destined to reach the United States—the *Cyane*—and the reason for this makes a separate story in itself.

After the action the vessels set sail for the island St. Jago, and entered the harbor of Porto Praya, having previously touched at one of the Cape Verd Islands.

On the 12th of March, as they lay at anchor under the guns of the neutral battery, three ships were discovered in the offing. Soon they were made out to be frigates, and the *Constitution* gave signal to get under way. No sooner had this happened than the forts on the shore commenced firing upon the Americans, and the British vessels hoisted the English colors. The *Constitution* and the *Levant* were standing on the wind to the southward and eastward, with all three of the enemy in chase. The *Cyane* bore up to the north, and shaped her course towards the United States. The *Levant*, a much slower sailer than the *Constitution*, kept falling behind, and Stewart saw that it would be foolishness to attempt to close with a force so much superior.

He signalled Lieutenant Ballard, the prize commander of the *Levant*, to make back to the harbor; she came about, made the entrance safely, and anchored in so close to the shore as to run her jibboom over the Portuguese battery; and the latter, as if to show her "neutrality" to the satisfaction of the English, cowardly fired upon her as she lay there, and, despite the fact that Ballard did not reply, but hauled down his flag, the *Acasta* and the *Newcastle*, two of the pursuers, came in and also fired at her a number of times. But, as if in poetic justice for the action of the Portuguese, they did more harm to the town than to the ship.

When the officer from the British squadron came on board the *Levant*, he advanced briskly to the quarter-deck, and, with no attempt to conceal his eagerness, exclaimed to Lieutenant Ballard, who there awaited him:

"Sir, I believe I have the honor of taking the sword of Captain Blakeley, commander of the American sloop of war the *Wasp*."

"No, sir," was the reply; "if you have an excess of pride in this case, you have the honor of receiving the sword of Captain Ballard, prize commander of His British Majesty's ship the *Levant*."

It was evident from the crestfallen appearance of the Britisher that he had expected a different reply. To receive the sword of Blakeley would have been a feather in his cap.

A strange state of things existed on board the *Constitution* as she sailed off to the west. She had on board no fewer than 240 prisoners, and the number of English officers who were unwilling guests was double that of her own. As this was the last cruise of the grand old ship in the second war with Great Britain, a short *résumé* of her career will be of interest:

Exclusive of the merchant vessels that had been

sent back to the United States, in her actions with armed vessels of the English navy she had taken 154 guns, made upwards of 900 prisoners, killed or wounded 298 of the enemy, and the value of the property captured could not be estimated at less than one and a half millions of dollars.

The strange discrepancy which existed between the loss of life on board of her and her antagonists is to be noted. In her action with the *Cyane* and the *Levant* she lost 3 killed and 13 wounded, while the killed and wounded on board her opponents, so far as could be ascertained, were 77.

Another interesting fact is that she has been in commission within the last twelve years, and only a few years ago she again breasted the waves, and was towed from the capes of the Delaware to her final resting-place in Massachusetts Bay.

# XVIII
# THE "HORNET" AND THE "PENGUIN"
[March 23d, 1815]

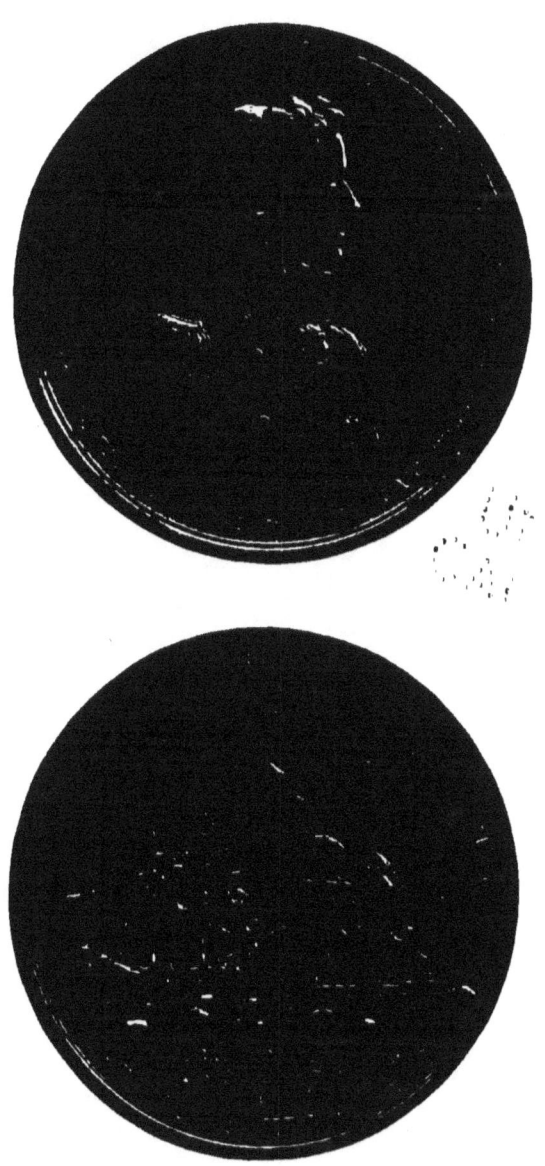

MEDAL PRESENTED BY CONGRESS TO
CAPTAIN JAMES BIDDLE

L IEUTENANT JAMES BIDDLE had distinguished himself in the Mediterranean in the war with the Barbary pirates, having been one of the officers captured with Captain Bainbridge on board the *Philadelphia*, and being, with Bainbridge, held prisoner during those historic months of captivity in Tripoli. Biddle was a young man of much determination, and his career as a junior officer was full of adventure and the successful overcoming of hardships. On the outbreak of the war of 1812 he sought every opportunity to be in the thick of it, neglecting no chance to distinguish himself or to add lustre to his name.

In the action between the *Wasp* and His British Majesty's sloop of war the *Frolic*, Biddle proved himself to have the proper spirit of a leader, and both he and Captain Jones were honored by Congress and the country after their short sojourn in an English prison; for it must be remembered that the *Wasp* and her prize were taken, within a few hours after their engagement, by a British seventy-four, the *Poictiers*.

Upon his return to the United States Biddle was promoted to the rank of captain, and at this time Captain James Lawrence, in consequence of his own promotion, had just left the sloop of war *Hornet*, which, under him, had fought so bravely and so fortunately in the southern seas. Captain Biddle asked for the command of the *Hornet* immediately upon Lawrence's leaving her—she was then lying in New York Harbor. His request was granted, and orders were given him to join his vessel with the frigate *Chesapeake*, then at Boston nearly ready for a cruise. But he and the brave Lawrence were never to make a voyage in company. News travelled slowly in those days, and young Captain Biddle went on with his preparations, sailing at last without hearing of the sad fate of his superior.

By the capture of the *Chesapeake*, however, all the signals and orders had fallen into the hands of the enemy. Immediately a frigate and several smaller vessels were sent out by the British to intercept the *Hornet*.

Captain Biddle had weighed anchor not alone, however, but in company with the frigates *United States* and *Macedonian*, going from New York through the Sound, as there was then a large British blockading force off Sandy Hook. The little American squadron was under the command of Commodore Decatur.

On the first day of June, within sight of Montauk Point, the three Yankee vessels were met by a larger and heavier force of the enemy. Decatur put back into the Sound and entered New London Harbor, closely pursued by the British, a ship of the line leading. In this chase the *Hornet*, being deep-laden and consequently slow, was nearly overtaken, being fired at by the two headmost ships at quite near range. The American vessels, going through Fisher's Island Sound, proceeded up the river Thames, and were moored across it, stem to stern, in order the better to defend themselves.

A long and tedious blockade now began, and Biddle's anxious spirit and courageous disposition fretted under the confinement. It was his first command; he was extremely anxious to measure his strength with an enemy whose force was equal to his own, and he tried again and again to obtain permission to make an attempt to elude the British squadron at the mouth of the river; but in this he failed, Decatur, his senior, forbidding him to risk the venture. For six long months no move was made by either side, although alarms were frequent.

Early in January, 1814, the blockading forces at New London were the *Ramillies* (74), Commodore Sir Thomas Hardy; the *Endymion*, Captain Hope; and the *Statira*, frigate, Captain Stackpole. There were also one or two smaller armed vessels within call. Upon one occasion an American prisoner of war, who was about to be landed at New London in exchange, was present during a conversation among the English officers, who, tired of acting as jailers, were anxious for a conflict. Upon landing he reported what he had heard to the Americans, and Captain Biddle, under a flag of truce, obtained an interview with Sir Thomas Hardy on board the *Ramillies*. He did his best to secure a meeting between the two frigates *United States* and the *Macedonian* on one side, and the *Endymion* and the *Statira* on the other.

Sir Thomas, after thinking the matter over, declined the meeting between the *Endymion* and the *United States* on account of the difference in force; the captain of the *Statira* did not wish to try it alone, and so the meeting fell through. And what a strange comment upon the pomp and circumstance of war! Biddle was so anxious himself to fight, and so trusted in the honor of the enemy, that, hearing that a British corvette was shortly to join the station, he would have sailed out through the hostile fleet in the *Hornet* to meet her all alone. It was the *Loup-Cervier* that was soon expected to arrive; this vessel had once been the tidy American sloop of war the *Wasp*, and Biddle had been second in command of her. Now, however, she was under a Captain Mends, and flew, instead of the "sailors' rights," the cross of St. George. However, after some correspondence, the meeting was given up, much to Biddle's chagrin, and the rechristened *Loup-Cervier* sailed out to sea after delivering despatches.

All through the winter a close blockade of New London was kept up, and it was found impossible to make any escape. At last the government ordered the two American frigates to be moved up the Thames as far as possible, and there they were dismantled. The officers and crew were transferred to other cities, while Captain Biddle was ordered to continue at New London for the protection of the shipping. In vain he protested against this hopeless and mortifying situation. The enemy made no serious preparations for trying to take the force up the river, and at last Biddle succeeded in obtaining permission to try to sail through the British fleet. Leaving the *United States* and the *Macedonian* protected by land batteries, he placed the *Hornet* in the best of trim, and on the night of the 18th of November, undiscovered, he drifted past the guard-ships and arrived safely at New York. It was seventeen months since he had been free.

Biddle was immediately attached, with his ship, to the command of Commodore Decatur again, and was ordered for a cruise to the East Indies. The frigate *President*, the flag-ship of the little squadron, went to sea on the 14th of January, 1815, and from the outset was pursued by the worst of misfortunes, that included shipwreck and final capture. On the 23d of January — not knowing of the loss of the *President*—the *Peacock*, the *Hornet*, and a store-vessel went out to sea in a gale of wind. Three days afterwards they separated, and, hearing of the *President's* fate from a merchantman, set out for themselves. Late in March, Biddle anchored near the headlands of Tristan d'Acunha, and on the 23d of the month, off the island, a sail was discovered to the southward and eastward. The *Hornet*, ever on the alert, raised anchor and bore up before the wind. When within five miles Biddle shortened sail and waited for the stranger to come down to him. It is quite amusing to think that the idea that was uppermost in the mind of the British commander (for it was H. M. S. *Penguin*, a heavily armed brig, that the *Hornet* had sighted) was this: that if the American saw who it was and how formidable was his ship, he would escape. So the Englishman concealed his identity as much as possible by clumsily taking in his sail to encourage Biddle to wait for him, carefully keeping bow on to the *Hornet* to hide his strength. Biddle, not understanding his intention, and the idea of running away being the last thing in the world for him to think about, was puzzled. He wore ship three times, trying to get the other to haul by the wind and to show his broadside, but without success. As the enemy approached nearly within musket-shot, the Englishman at last hauled on the starboard tack and hoisted his colors, firing a challenging gun. Biddle immediately luffed, flew his ensign, and gave the enemy a broadside. It was then about forty minutes past one. The action became brisk, and in fifteen minutes the Englishman came down again, bow foremost, as if he would fall on board the *Hornet*. Orders were given to prepare to repel the expected boarders, but the men could scarcely be restrained from tumbling over the bow of the *Penguin* as her jib-boom crossed the *Hornet's* taffrail.

There was a considerable swell, the sea lifted the *Hornet* ahead, and the bowsprit of the enemy (her men had displayed no intention of boarding) carried away the mizzen-shrouds and swept the side. Just then an officer bravely stood upon the bulwarks of the English brig, and at the risk of his life shouted out that he had surrendered. He was Lieutenant McDonald, the *Penguin's* first lieutenant. At this moment the enemy was swinging clear, Biddle was prepared to give him another broadside, and with difficulty could he restrain his crew, as the *Penguin* certainly had fired after Lieutenant McDonald had said he had surrendered. One of the last shots had struck Captain Biddle, wounding him severely in the neck. In fact, throughout the action he was almost unrecognizable, because of wounds which he had received from splinters in his face. Several times his men had asked him to go below.

It was exactly twenty-two minutes from the beginning of the action to the time when the *Penguin* was boarded by a boat from the *Hornet*. The former vessel proved to be one of the strongest vessels of her class, mounting 16 32-pound carronades, 2 long sixes, and a 12-pound carronade on her topgallant forecastle, with swivels on the capstan and in the tops; she had a spare port forward so as to fire both of her long guns on a side. When she had sailed from England on the 1st of September she was manned by a picked crew, that was afterwards reinforced by marines taken from the *Medway*, a seventy-four. Out of one hundred and thirty-two persons that formed her crew she lost fourteen killed and twenty-eight wounded, among the latter number being her commander, Captain Dickinson. Not a single round shot struck the hull of the *Hornet*, but her sides were filled with grape and her sails and rigging much cut. She had but one man killed and eleven wounded. The *Penguin* was so badly riddled that she sank, it not being worth the while to attempt to save her. But the *Hornet*, after obtaining a new set of sails, was ready for service without going home for repairs or refitting. The English journals, in commenting on this fact, advocated strongly the adoption of the American system of gunnery instruction, to which a Baltimore paper replied that the only thing they (the British) needed to be taught was " to *shoot* Yankee fashion—viz., straighter and more often."

THE "PENGUIN" STRIKES TO THE "HORNET"

# XIX
## THE ESCAPE OF THE "HORNET"
[April 29th, 1815]

ALTHOUGH the treaty of peace between England and the United States was concluded at Ghent on November 24th, in the year 1814, hostilities continued even after the *signing* of the document that took place a month later to a day.

This can be well understood when we stop to think that at the best rates of travelling it would take in the neighborhood of three weeks, or possibly four, for the news to reach the United States.

The battle of New Orleans, so disastrous to the English arms, would never have taken place if there had been such a thing as a cable in those days. Nor would there have occurred several smart actions at sea, including, sad to relate, the capture of the U. S. S. *President* by a British squadron.

There is no excuse, however, for the long detention of American prisoners in the hands of the British, when there was no longer any chance of their serving against her.

On February 17th President Madison ratified the Treaty of Ghent, and hostilities practically ceased, although, of course, not knowing this fact, Captain Stewart, in command of the *Constitution*, captured the *Cyane* and the *Levant*, two British sloops of war.

And on the 23d of March, on a foreign station, the gallant Captain Biddle, in command of the *Hornet*, captured and sank the *Penguin*.

. But even so long past the time when the news might have been expected to be about the world, on April 27th, 1815, off the Island of San Salvador, the sloop of war *Hornet* had the last hostile experience with the English of that eventful period. The little sloop was sailing in company with the *Peacock*, and together they made a pair of fighters that were not afraid of anything that carried in the neighborhood of their weight of metal.

In a letter from Biddle, the senior captain, to Stephen Decatur appears the following: "The *Peacock* and this ship, having continued off Tristan d'Acunha the number of days directed by you in your letter of instruction, proceeded in company to the eastward on the twelfth day of April, bound to the second place of rendezvous. Nothing of any importance occurred until the twenty-second day of April at 7 A.M., in latitude 38° 30' and longitude 33' east. The wind was from northeast by north and light through the day, and by sundown we had neared the chase considerably. It was calm during the day, and at daylight on the 28th he [Warrington of the *Peacock*] was not in sight. A breeze springing from the northwest, we crowded steering sails on both sides, and the chase was made out standing to the northward upon a wind. At 2.45 P.M. the *Peacock* was about six miles ahead of this ship, and, observing that she appeared to be suspicious of the chase, I took in starboard steering-sails and hauled up for the *Peacock*. I was still, however, of opinion that the chase was an Indiaman, though, indeed, the atmosphere was quite smoky and indistinct, and I concluded she was very large. Captain Warrington was waiting for me to join him, that we might get together alongside of her. At 3.22 P.M. the *Peacock* made the signal that the chase was a ship of the line and an enemy. I took in immediately all steering-sails and hauled upon the wind, the enemy being then upon our lee quarter, distant about eight miles. By sundown I had perceived that the enemy sailed remarkably fast and was very weatherly." . . .

This letter was dated from San Salvador, June 10th, 1815.

It had been very calm on the morning of the 28th when the great ship had been sighted which, as Biddle has recorded, every one took to be a large East-Indiaman. As the *Peacock* was in advance and to the windward of the stranger, it was feared by the crew of the *Hornet* that she would be first to place herself alongside and secure the rich prize. According to the private journal of one of the officers on the *Hornet*, they had already begun in their imagination to divide the contents of the vessel they expected to capture among them. If she came from the Indies, the sailors declared that they would carpet the berth-deck with costly rugs; while if she hailed from England and was on an outward voyage, the officers revelled in the idea of what her larder might contain; the probable value of her cargo was estimated carefully.

The *Hornet* was crowding on all sail in order to draw up before the *Peacock* should have had the best of the picking. Captain Biddle was on deck with his glass in hand watching the *Peacock*, when suddenly he saw her swing about (she was well to windward), and fly a signal telling that the big vessel was a ship of the line. The *Peacock* was a faster sailer than the *Hornet*, as the latter sat deep in the water, and, owing to the weight of metal she carried, was slow in stays. But it was evident, by six o'clock in the evening, three hours after Warrington had signalled Biddle to beware of approaching nearer, that the big fellow had turned the tables and was evidently the pursuer, with the intention of running down the *Hornet*. Every minute the sails rose higher and higher above the horizon until the great hull was in plain view. She weathered the little *Hornet*, and it was seen that at the rate of progress the two were making the seventy-four would be within gunshot sometime during the night.

Immediately the wedges of the lower masts were loosened, and at nine o'clock orders were given to lighten ship as much as possible. The sheet-anchor was cut away and hove overboard, and all of the cable followed it. Then the spare rigging and spars were put over the side, and before ten o'clock they scuttled the wardroom-deck and hove overboard about fifty tons of the kentledge.

It was a bright night, with all the stars shining, and there was no use disguising the matter: the *Hornet* was continually dropping back. The seventy-four fired a gun and signalled, but Biddle did not respond. Like Hull, who brought the *Constitution* successfully away from a superior force, by pluck and attention to duty, knowledge and seamanship, he determined to leave nothing untried that would tend to increase the rate of his vessel's sailing.

At two in the morning the *Hornet* tacked to the southward and westward, and immediately the enemy astern did likewise. At daylight the line-of-battle ship was within gunshot on the *Hornet's* lee quarter. At seven in the morning the English colors were displayed at the peak of the Britisher, and a rear-admiral's flag was flown at his mizzen-topgallant mast-head. At the same time he began firing from his bow guns—it must be assumed more as an imperious order for the *Hornet* to show her colors and heave to than with an idea of crippling her, for the shot overreached her about a mile.

Biddle paid no attention at all, but having ascertained that the lightening of his ship made her much faster, he went at it again, cutting away the remaining anchors, and letting every foot of cable go overboard. Then he broke up the launch and left the débris in the wake. Even the provisions were broken into, and barrels of salt-horse and bread thrown out upon the waters. Then more kentledge followed, and, tapping the magazines, he threw over all but a dozen or so of round shot. Then over went the capstan, which was no easy job, and they began on the guns; one after another they plashed overboard. All this time the *Cornwallis*, the great seventy-four, kept up a continual firing, to which no reply was made. In fact, for four hours the English gunners displayed the worst marksmanship on record, for their shot continually went ahead of and all around the *Hornet* without once striking her, although several passed between her masts.

At eleven the breeze began to freshen, and the seventy-four commenced to creep up slowly, and then gain all at once in a manner which caused Biddle to believe that the Englishman had made alterations in his trim. By noon the wind had shifted slightly, and was squally, with fresh breezes from the westward. It was Sunday, the 30th, but there was no service held. Gloom was everywhere throughout the American vessel: staring them in the face were apparently inevitable capture and the frightful confinement in an English prison. Many of the crew had already been impressed and had served in the English navy, escaping from time to time, and the idea of being held as deserters—deserters to a country that was not theirs—gave cause for much unhappiness. At 1 P.M. the *Cornwallis* was so close that her commander began to fire by divisions, and once let go his entire broadside loaded with round and grape. But, as is recorded in the journal, "the former passed between our masts and the latter fell all around us. The enemy fired shells, but they were so ill directed as to be perfectly harmless." And now began what looked to be a work of destruction, and which was intended as such, no doubt. Biddle determined that if he were taken there would be very little for the enemy to show as trophy. Overboard went all the muskets, cutlasses, and ironwork. The bell was broken up, and the topgallant forecastle was chopped to pieces. All this time only three-quarters of a mile on the lee quarter was the great ship of the line pouring in a constant storm of shot and shell. The Yankee tars trimmed ship by massing themselves against the rail, after the fashion of a yacht's crew.

At four o'clock a shot from the enemy struck the jib-boom, and another caught the starboard bulwark just forward of the gangway. A third smashed on the deck forward of the main-hatch, and, glancing up, passed through the foresail. It struck immediately over the head of a wounded Yankee sailor who had been hurt in the action with the *Penguin;* the splinters were scattered all around the invalid, and a small paper flag, the American ensign, that he had hoisted over his cot, was struck down. But immediately he lifted it up and waved it about his head. In fact, to quote again from the entry in the journal, " Destruction stared us in the face if we did not surrender, yet no officer, no man in the ship, showed any disposition to let the enemy have the poor little *Hornet.*"

Captain Biddle mustered the crew, and told them that, as they might soon be captured, he hoped to perceive that propriety of conduct that had distinguished them, and that he was pleased at being their commander. But now, as if by a miracle, the *Hornet* began to gain. The wind blew more aft, and by five the enemy's shot fell short. Biddle had not replied even with his stern-chaser to all this cannonading, for he had noticed that the other's firing hampered her sailing. At half-past five the crew broke out into a cheer, for the *Cornwallis* was dropping behind, slowly, but surely. Now Biddle showed his colors, and so fast did the *Hornet* pick up, with the wind in her favorite quarter for good going, that a few minutes after six the enemy was hull down. All night long the distance between the two increased, and at daylight the *Cornwallis* was fifteen miles behind. At nine o'clock she shortened sail, hauled upon the wind to the eastward, and gave up, after a chase of forty-two hours.

A remarkable circumstance of this affair is that, owing to the variableness of the wind, the *Hornet* had made a perfect circle around the battle-ship.

The relief occasioned to all by the escape was vented in cheering, and, extra grog being passed, the men were in extremely good temper, despite the fact of their precarious condition, for they were on the high seas with no guns, no boats, no anchors, and short of provisions. They had packed up all their things, thinking that they would soon have to go on board the enemy as prisoners, but now, joyfully, they returned them to their places.

In the fine writing of the period that every person who touched pen and ink seemed prone to, the author of the journal says: "This was truly a glorious victory over the horrors of banishment and the terrors of a British floating dungeon. Quick as thought, every face was changed from the gloom of despair to the highest smile of delight, and we began once more to breathe the sweets of liberty. The bitter sighs of regret were now changed."

Biddle asked and obtained a court of inquiry to investigate the matter of his throwing overboard almost everything but the skin of his vessel, and on the 23d of August, 1815, by order of the Secretary of the Navy, court was convened on board the *Hornet*, and the following opinion was pronounced: " The court, after mature deliberation on the testimony adduced, are of opinion that no blame is imputable to Captain Biddle on account of the return of the *Hornet* into port with the loss of her armament, stores, etc., and that the greatest applause is due to him for his persevering gallantry and nautical skill, evinced in escaping, under the most disadvantageous circumstance, after a long and arduous chase by a British line-of-battle ship."

The *Cornwallis* fired the last gunshot of the war of 1812.

www.ingramcontent.com/pod-product-compliance
Lightning Source LLC
Chambersburg PA
CBHW030017240426
43672CB00007B/993